STORIES
OF
WORDS
AND
PHRASES

Sumanto Chattopadhyay is the creator of The English Nut, an award-winning social media channel focused on the nuances of the English language. Through it, he has enlightened and entertained viewers with weekly videos about vocabulary and etymology, grammar and usage since 2019. He has written many articles on advertising, English, travel and other subjects for various Indian periodicals. He is an international-award-winning advertising copywriter. His work has won awards at the Cannes Lions, the Clios, the One Show, the London International Awards, the Effies, the ABBYs, the Kyoorius Design Awards and elsewhere. He is also an actor and was nominated for the best actor award at the Filmmaker Festival of World Cinema in Nice, France.

'Words and phrases have stories to tell—often unexpected, sometimes amusing, always revealing. Sumanto listens closely, following them through history and across continents, uncovering their curious origins with affection and wit. This book is a delightful exploration for those who love the English language and its many surprises.'

—**Ruskin Bond**

STORIES OF WORDS AND PHRASES

Discover the fascinating stories behind everyday expressions

Sumanto Chattopadhyay
(creator of 'The English Nut')

RUPA

Published by
Rupa Publications India Pvt. Ltd 2025
161-B/4, Gulmohar House,
Yusuf Sarai Community Centre,
New Delhi 110049

Sales centres:
Bengaluru Chennai
Hyderabad Kolkata Mumbai

Copyright © Sumanto Chattopadhyay 2025

The views and opinions expressed in this book are the author's own and the facts are as reported by him which have been verified to the extent possible, and the publishers are not in any way liable for the same.

All rights reserved.
No part of this publication may be reproduced, transmitted or stored in a retrieval system, in any form or by any means, electronic, mechanical, photocopying, recording or otherwise, without the prior permission of the publisher.

P-ISBN: 978-93-7003-418-1
E-ISBN: 978-93-7003-183-8

Second impression 2025

10 9 8 7 6 5 4 3 2

The moral right of the author has been asserted.

Printed in India

This book is sold subject to the condition that it shall not, by way of trade or otherwise, be lent, resold, hired out or otherwise circulated, without the publisher's prior consent, in any form of binding or cover other than that in which it is published.

*To my parents, Arati and Gouranga Chattopadhyay,
with whom this journey began.*

∽

Contents

Foreword by Dr Shashi Tharoor — xi
Introduction — xv

STORIES OF WORDS

1. Blockbuster — 3
2. Phoney — 7
3. Pedigree — 11
4. Basketball — 13
5. Lunatic — 17
6. Malaria — 19
7. Sideburn — 21
8. Limerick — 23
9. Quarantine — 28
10. Deadline — 30
11. Boycott — 32
12. Gossip — 35
13. Braille — 39
14. Sinister — 41
15. Thug / Loot / Dacoit — 44
16. Cannibal / Avocado / Chilli — 47
17. Bluetooth / Ritzy / Sandwich / Silhouette — 49
18. Safari / Orange / Algebra — 52
19. Machiavellian — 54
20. Indigo — 56
21. Lemon — 59
22. Pagoda — 63
23. Adonis — 66
24. Chess — 70

25. Ammonia	73
26. Sardonic	76
27. Mesmerize	79
28. Khaki	83
29. Berserk	87
30. Assassin	90

STORIES OF PHRASES

31. Teddy bear	97
32. White elephant	100
33. Caught red-handed	104
34. Blue blood	107
35. Cost an arm and a leg	111
36. An apple a day keeps the doctor away	114
37. Play it by ear	117
38. Bite the bullet	120
39. Crocodile tears	123
40. Cat got your tongue?	126
41. Get your goat	128
42. Break a leg	131
43. Barking up the wrong tree	134
44. Wolf in sheep's clothing	137
45. Elementary, my dear Watson	140
46. Green-eyed monster	142
47. Murphy's law	146
48. A dish fit for the gods	150
49. If they have no bread, let them eat cake	153
50. One fell swoop	157
51. Dead ringer / Saved by the bell / Graveyard shift	160
52. Hair of the dog / Let the cat out of the bag	165
53. Hot-blooded	170
54. Red herring	173

55.	Ears are burning	177
56.	Wear your heart on your sleeve / Foam at the mouth	180
57.	A bird in hand is worth two in the bush / Straight from the horse's mouth	184
58.	In stitches (and other related expressions)	187
59.	Cold shoulder	191
60.	It's raining cats and dogs	194
61.	Keeping up with the Joneses	197
62.	Beating about the bush / Nineteen to the dozen	200
63.	Steal someone's thunder / Silver lining	204
64.	Can't hold a candle to	208
65.	Close, but no cigar	210
66.	In the limelight	213
67.	Push the envelope / Make the grade	216
68.	Have your work cut out / Get the sack	219
69.	Pull out all the stops / Pass the buck	223
70.	Mad as a hatter	227
71.	Once in a blue moon	229
72.	Don't throw the baby out with the bathwater	233
73.	Run amok / Run-of-the-mill	236
74.	Rest on your laurels	240
75.	A flash in the pan	243
76.	Goody two-shoes	246
77.	Read the riot act / As pleased as Punch	250
78.	Mind your p's and q's / Fly off the handle	254
79.	Extend an olive branch	258
80.	Red tape / It's Greek to me	261

Acknowledgements   265
References   267

Foreword

A few years ago, when I sat down with Sumanto Chattopdhyay—known and loved by netizens as The English Nut, the friendly neighbourhood English language obsessive—I quickly realized that he is no snob in matters linguistic, nor is he an Anglophile. All too often in India, loving English is looked upon as a sin worthy of perdition: you love English and its literature? Well, then you are likely to be sneered at and, through gritted teeth, told that you are a relic the British left behind to look down, as they once had, on those of your fellow Indians who cannot speak English as well as you. Such derision is all the more strident and searing if, instead of belonging to an elite section of Indian society, you happen to be middle class. Because what right, then, have you, or so the logic goes, to be proficient in English or claim to love its literature? Also, as eyes narrow and brows furrow, you are charged with being deracinated—because, surely, you must be cut off from your roots and disdainful of your national and civilizational heritage if you love English, right?

Wrong. As an Indian writer of both fiction and non-fiction in English, I have argued for as long as I can remember that language is largely a vehicle, meant to carry your readers to the destination you wish to transport them to. Just as a car designed and manufactured in Germany or the United States or Japan can bestride Indian roads with aplomb, so too can an authentically Indian tale—or voice—transmute itself into English and spill forth onto the page, to be comprehended as unmistakably Indian, as wholly *desi*, as the works of many postcolonial Indian authors writing in English, including mine, have been. Lest we forget, this is also a tongue in which we wrested our country back from British thraldom, marshalling English in our crusade against Englishmen and striking back at the Empire in its own language. This was an enterprise helmed by R.C. Dutt, Dinshaw Wacha and Dadabhai Naoroji in the late nineteenth century, and Mahatma Gandhi and Jawaharlal Nehru in the twentieth. We Indians, let us never forget, have long had a penchant to Indianize all things foreign, and this we have done not only with cuisines (such as Chinese, since Indian Chinese is a sizzling breed of its own), but also languages—in particular English, with Indian English transmogrifying a colonial remnant into a pragmatic and utilitarian tool for effective communication. While I have roundly debunked the notion that English was a gift of an enlightened British despotism in my book *An Era of Darkness: The British Empire in India*, one cannot overlook some of its positive upshots. Foremost among these are its roles as a conduit for knowledge and a great bridge, interlinking Indians from different regions of our enormous nation and, simultaneously, India with the world at large, allowing us to play many an indispensable role on the international stage.

Sumanto understands this, of course. Back in 2019, when he first slipped on the persona of The English Nut and began making weekly videos—decidedly whimsical and witty—on the nuances of the English language, on vocabulary and etymology, grammar and syntax, he was merely channelling an irrepressible curiosity, which had defined him since his earliest days, into a new avenue. Here, he and others like him (and I plead guilty to belonging to their ranks!) could together examine—and exult in—the foibles of English. Over the years, this etymological egghead has entertained, enlightened, educated and enriched countless Indians, among them many youngsters, with the wonders of this language. Whereas I, as a child, built up my vocabulary by indiscriminate reading—encountering a new word in different contexts and deducing what it means—Sumanto (enamoured of the newness of a word hitherto unseen and unheard) would start guessing what it might mean. He would then rush to his parents, demanding to know whether his guesses were accurate. Thus was planted the seedling that would, in time, blossom into The English Nut. Yet, for Sumanto, it was never words for their own sake, or for the sake of constructing a formidable vocabulary. Instead, as he evocatively writes, words became for him 'not just carriers of meaning but tiny time capsules, preserving within themselves fragments of history, culture and human ingenuity.'

Words and their origins, language and its numberless uses: these are for Sumanto reminders that language, with which our paths to each other's minds and hearts are paved, 'is a lens through which we view the world, and that lens is constantly being polished, scratched and refashioned.' Therefore, to examine a language and the words and rules—of grammar, syntax, and so on—that mould it is to behold, in whichever age and part of the world you may be, the ceaseless passage of time, the endless turning of the wheel of history.

'Language,' writes Sumanto, 'is not static; it breathes, it grows, it adapts.' This is especially true of English, which has long been an ever-flowing stream, washing over the shores of numerous nations—thanks largely to British colonialism, which in time placed it at the heart of globalization and international diplomacy—and imbibing words, idioms and expressions from vastly diverse, often disparate, cultures: from Persian to French, Hindi to Latin, Greek to German. Today, far from being an arsenal under British control, English is a linguistic potpourri, resonant with the echoes and refrains of every civilization it has ever come into contact with. But even though it is a kaleidoscopic reflection of an ever-intermingling world, this fact is largely lost on us. Thankfully, Sumanto is here with this delightful volume, *Stories of Words and Phrases*, to remind us of this.

Writing that words 'are windows into the cultural and historical forces that shaped language, and us,' Sumanto beckons us to join him on an exhilarating voyage down the warrens of time and history, where we encounter not only words but entire cultures and civilizations, and where we are whisked across the globe not in aircraft or trains but by that greatest vehicle of all time—language. In doing so, Sumanto brings us face to face with facets of our world we are oblivious to. Far from being a sedate examination of the origins of the words we commonly use—mistakenly believing that they have been part of English all along—this is an exciting and informative chronicle of how some of the most popular and commonplace English words and phrases acquired their meanings. Indeed, as Sumanto leads us to discover, many of them have no relation whatsoever with anything Anglo-Saxon! As this wonderful word guide writes: 'What's fascinating is how these words and phrases, once bound to specific contexts, have transcended their original meanings.'

All in all, Sumanto endeavours to inform us not only of where the words we use—and take for granted—come from, but also of where they *lead us*. These words, says he, 'reveal the shared human experience that underpins the English language, linking us to generations past, present and future.' In his inimitably curious and companionable way, Sumanto Chattopadhyay reminds us that every word we utter carries echoes of history, culture and human imagination—of civilizations lost and those yet to be discovered. Thus, *Stories of Words and Phrases* is not merely a probe into the origins of modern English, but also—and more important—a testament to our shared history and shared stories, to relate and record which we devised language, one word at a time.

Dr Shashi Tharoor

Introduction

Ever since I was a child, I would greet any new word or phrase that I came across with a joyful sense of curiosity. I would try to guess its meaning and origin. Then I would go to my parents to see if my guesswork was accurate.

My parents quickly introduced me to the dictionary—so that I could do my own spadework. And thus began my journey of discovering the stories of words and phrases.

It turned into a lifelong habit. Words became for me not just carriers of meaning but tiny time capsules, preserving within themselves fragments of history, culture and human ingenuity.

I was captivated by the way language evolved—how some words retained their old essence while others morphed beyond recognition; how phrases that once belonged to warriors and poets slipped into everyday conversation, often without us being aware of their storied pasts.

Some years ago, I decided to create an alter ego that would be dedicated to bringing these stories to the public. Thus, The English Nut, my social media persona and channel, was born. It is focused on the nuances of the English language, aiming to educate and entertain viewers with weekly videos about vocabulary, etymology, grammar and usage. What started as a simple passion project—a way to share my love for words—soon found an audience of fellow 'verbivores'. Together we celebrated language for its quirks, its unpredictability and its depth.

Then Rupa Publications approached The English Nut to turn this endeavour into a book. And so began the long process of writing, editing and incubation. There were words and phrases to be researched, origins to be verified and cultural references to be found. Every entry in this book has been chosen not just for its etymological intrigue but also for the engaging stories connected to it.

In shaping this collection, I came to see more clearly how language, like a river, meanders through time, carrying with it the sediment of human experience. Words and phrases are not static artefacts but living, breathing entities—shaped by societal change, technological advancement, political shifts and cultural fusions.

Take the word 'boycott', for instance. It originated from the name of Captain Charles Boycott, a land agent in nineteenth-century Ireland who was socially ostracized during a rent dispute. His name soon became a verb, and now we use it without any thought of Irish tenant farmers or Victorian-era landlords. Or consider 'khaki', which entered English through colonial India, borrowed from the Persian-Urdu word for 'dusty'—initially a practical colour for military uniforms, and now a fashion staple across the globe.

Every word in our vocabulary bears the imprint of history—some crossroads of trade, some battlefield, some scientific breakthrough or some work of art. The evolution of language is also the evolution of thought. When we trace a word back to its roots, we often uncover not just the story of the word, but also the story of the people who used it and the times they lived in.

The word 'assassin', for example, can be traced back to a sect of medieval warriors called the Hashashin, who were reputed to consume hashish before carrying out targeted killings. And the modern word 'mesmerize' is born from the name of Franz Mesmer, the German physician who practised a form of hypnotic therapy in the eighteenth century. These examples are windows into the cultural and historical forces that shaped language, and us.

I relied on many sources for the information in this book. Notable among them are *Phrase Finder*, *Word Histories*, *World Wide Words*, *Etymonline*, *Grammarphobia*, the *Encyclopaedia Britannica*, the *Oxford English Dictionary*, the *Cambridge Dictionary*, the *Collins Dictionary* and the *Merriam-Webster* dictionary. Primary sources were not always accessible—because of how old they are—so I used these reputed secondary sources (which are written or vetted by etymologists). I further confirmed the veracity of the information by cross-referencing multiple sources. Besides these references, I consulted various books and periodicals that are too numerous to mention here but are listed at the end. I also wish to note here that etymological theories constantly evolve as new information and older examples of the usage of a word or phrase come to light. So, what I have done in the book is mention the credible etymological theories, as well as a few interesting but discredited ones, so you can appreciate how the origin stories evolve over time—just like language itself.

Language is not static; it breathes, it grows, it adapts. Some words in this book have travelled across continents, carried by traders, explorers and conquerors ('cannibal' from the Caribbean, 'loot' from India and 'pagoda' from Persia). Others have leapt from the pages of literature (Shakespeare's 'green-eyed monster' or Sir Walter Scott's 'cold shoulder'). Some were names or nicknames of people ('silhouette', 'braille', 'Bluetooth'), others were born of antiquated practices ('red herring', 'bite the bullet'). And a few have origins so peculiar—words like 'avocado' and 'sardonic', and phrases like 'hair of the dog' and 'mad as a hatter'— that they seem almost too strange to be true!

What's fascinating is how these words and phrases, once bound to specific contexts, have transcended their original meanings. 'Deadline', for instance, began as a literal line that prisoners couldn't cross without risking being shot. Now it simply means 'a due date'. 'Gossip', once meaning 'godmother', has shifted to refer to idle or salacious chatter. 'Bluetooth', originally the nickname of a tenth-century Danish king, now connects our phones to our earbuds. These transformations remind us that language is a lens through which we view the world, and that lens is constantly being polished, scratched and refashioned.

But this book is not just about where certain English words come from—it is also about where they take us. They reveal the shared human experience that underpins the English language, linking us to generations past, present and future.

I hope this book sparks in you the same curiosity and delight that words and phrases have always sparked in me. May it offer you not just knowledge but also the thrill of uncovering something unexpected, something preposterous and something marvellous in the everyday words we take for granted.

So, turn the page, and let's begin.

Stories of Words

1

Blockbuster

The word 'blockbuster' usually refers to a movie, play, book, video game or any other product that is exceptionally popular and a huge commercial success—as in, a megahit. The term also implies that it is a big-budget production, specifically made and marketed to be a superhit.

Blockbuster. Doesn't the word have an explosive sound to it? This makes sense given that it originally referred to a huge aerial bomb, weighing 2,000 kilograms or more, which could bust or destroy an entire city block! The term originated in World War II, when such bombs were used by the Allied powers to bomb Nazi-occupied territories.

The word's first appearance in the American *TIME* magazine is in a 1942 article on the Allied bombing of key targets in Fascist Italy. The word transitioned quickly from being used in its military sense to being applied to things like sports and politics and then to entertainment. In 1943, *TIME* magazine used the word again, this time to describe a movie—not its box office success, but its content. It described the film *Mission to Moscow* as being 'as explosive as a blockbuster', which was still close to the original meaning of the word. The same year, advertisements in movie trade journals like *Variety* and *Motion Picture Herald* called the film *Bombardier* 'the block-buster of all action-thrill-service shows!' Another trade ad, from 1944, boasted that *With the Marines at Tarawa*, the war documentary, 'hits the heart like a two-ton blockbuster'.

Note that in the early days, blockbuster was often written as a hyphenated word, such as in the *Bombardier* ad. The hyphen was soon dropped though.

One of the earliest uses of blockbuster in the modern sense of a superhit film was in 1950, when the British *Daily Mirror* used it to describe the movie *Samson and Delilah* (1949). The movie was a romantic biblical drama directed by Cecil B. DeMille, one of the most influential filmmakers in history. The film depicted the biblical story of Samson, a warrior whose magical strength was rooted in his uncut hair. He fell in love with Delilah, who beguiled him into revealing the secret of his strength, had his hair cut while he slept, and betrayed him to his enemies.

The following year, in 1951, the word blockbuster was used in *Variety* to describe another classic film, *Quo Vadis*. A piece in the journal called the film a 'blockbuster' that was 'right up there with [...] *Gone With the Wind* for box office performance.'

Quo Vadis was an epic historical drama adapted from the 1896 international bestselling novel of the same name, written by the Polish Nobel Laureate Henryk Sienkiewicz. 'Quo vadis' is Latin for 'Where are you going?' It refers to an incident described in early Christian literature in which Peter the Apostle asks Jesus, 'Quo vadis?' As an aside, it is interesting to note that the Italian superstar Sophia Loren appeared as an uncredited extra in this film. The movie was number one at the US box office in 1951 and grossed US$30 million within the country. It was, indeed, a blockbuster in every sense of the word, as it reportedly saved MGM from bankruptcy.

Two years later, in 1953, when 135 Hollywood releases earned $1 million or more, *Variety* described it as 'a year of box-office blockbusters'. This marked the cementing of the modern sense of the word in popular parlance.

To use the language of screenplay, let's cut to 1975, when the iconic film *Jaws* was released. Steven Spielberg's thriller was about a man-eating great white shark that attacks beachgoers at a resort town. The local police chief goes after the shark with the help of a marine biologist and a professional shark hunter, resulting in many blood-curdling scenes!

This movie redefined the blockbuster—or rather, defined the 'summer blockbuster'—and became the highest-grossing film of all time. Until, of course, it was surpassed by the epic *Star Wars* (1977) two years later!

The super successful run of *Jaws* was regarded as a watershed moment in cinema history. Along with films like *Star Wars* and *Alien* (1979), which followed later, *Jaws* established the 'summer blockbuster' genre, loosely defined as films that are released in the summer when colleges and schools are on a break in the US. Such blockbusters typically do exceptional business at the box office.

Now let's cut to a subplot about a completely different meaning of blockbuster, unrelated to the entertainment business. This usage dates back to 1955. It refers to a real estate broker or speculator who sells a house in an all-white neighbourhood to an African-American family, leading to an exodus of white families, causing housing prices to decline. The broker then profits from this racism-driven market instability. This practice is called blockbusting and the person who perpetrates it is called a blockbuster. I don't know which is worse—this money-making racket or the racism that makes it possible.

Coming back to Hollywood and *Jaws*, here is an interesting piece of trivia: Spielberg wanted to shoot an additional scene, but the studio refused to pay for it. The rest of the movie had already been shot in and by the ocean at a place called Martha's Vineyard. But now the director had to improvise in a swimming pool in Encino, California. A latex model of the character, whose head is found bitten off by the shark in the film, was created. And the murky waters off Martha's Vineyard were recreated by pouring milk powder into the pool! Had the real shark been in the pool, I wonder if it would have enjoyed consuming the reconstituted milk with a dash of chlorine instead of the humans it had developed a taste for!

Indian cinema too has its share of blockbusters. People tend to equate Indian cinema with Bollywood—the Mumbai-centred Hindi film industry—but many films are made in the so-called regional languages in other parts of the country. And some of the biggest blockbusters of recent years have come from those movie industries. The Telugu-language films *Baahubali* (2015) and *Baahubali 2* (2017) are two of them, the second one being the bigger hit. The film *2.0* (2018) is a Tamil-language blockbuster starring the South Indian megastar Rajinikanth in a 'triple role'. Of course, Bollywood isn't short on blockbusters either. Three of them are associated with Aamir Khan—*Dangal* (2016), *PK* (2014) and *Secret Superstar* (2017)—while a fourth, *Bajrangi Bhaijaan* (2015), stars Salman Khan.

2

Phoney

This chapter is all about the word 'phoney'—or 'p-h-o-n-y', as the Americans write it.

Meaning 'sham', 'counterfeit' or 'insincere', phoney sounds like it is related to the word 'phone'. There is even a theory that the word originated during the period when telephones first became widely used. People feared that they might be deceived by fraudulent calls—from 'phoney' people—and that supposedly led to the invention of the word. This seems entirely plausible against today's backdrop, when vishing or voice phishing has become a thriving industry, and we frequently receive phone calls purportedly from our bank asking us for our secret codes to complete some formality or the other.

I recently got a call, supposedly from an insurance company. I had invested money in a policy some years ago, they said. The policy had become inactive because I had not paid the annual instalments. But if I paid up now, I would get a hefty return. A call to the actual insurance company helpline confirmed that no policy with that number existed. In hindsight, I'm glad I was circumspect about this call, as it turned out to be a phoney one.

On a related note, let us do a quick review of con vocabulary: 'con' is a slang abbreviation for 'confidence', as in 'con artist', 'con game' or 'con trick'. To con people is to defraud them by exploiting their naïveté, compassion, vanity or greed, after winning their confidence.

A con artist—or swindler—is the person who perpetrates

this crime. The swindle itself is called a con game—though of course for the victim—known as the 'mark' or 'dupe' in con terminology—it is no game at all. Con is also a slang abbreviation for 'convict', which is what the con artist becomes if he or she gets caught.

Coming back to the word phoney, it was introduced in the late nineteenth century, a couple of decades after the first telephone call was made—but the words are not related. So, if not from phone, where does phoney come from?

The most credible theory is that it comes from the word 'fawney', which is part of the name of the old confidence trick called the 'fawney rig'—which has nothing to do with fawning.

This is how Francis Grose's *A Classical Dictionary of the Vulgar Tongue* (second edition, 1788) describes the fawney rig: 'A common fraud, thus practised: A fellow drops a brass ring, double gilt, which he picks up before the party meant to be cheated, and to whom he disposes of it for less than its supposed, and ten times more than its real, value.'

The *Dictionary of Crime* by Jay Robert Nash provides further detail:

> The confidence man would drop a Lady's purse containing a cheap ring and wait for someone to spot it. He would then pretend to notice at the same time and claim half the loot for sharing in the discovery. The confidence man or an accomplice would appraise the ring at three or four times its real value, and offer the dupe his half of the find for about double its actual value.

The con man who practised this finger-ring con was known as the 'fawney man'.

Those days, a London shop specializing in fake gold rings did good business as a 'fawney factory'. Even today, knowingly or unknowingly, people buy and wear fake gold rings. A well-known Indian jeweller once put on a fashion show with fake gold. He hired uniformed security personnel for the event to con people into believing that the gold jewellery was genuine! That is taking fawney or phoney to the next level!

The word fawney came from the Irish word 'fainne', meaning 'finger ring'. 'Rig' means 'trick' or 'swindle'. Irish confidence tricksters—or fawney men—probably brought the 'fawney rig' to England. The term also travelled to America with Irish immigrants. It was in the US that 'fawney' transformed into 'phony', and by the end of the nineteenth century, it became a popular term in horseracing to describe fraudulent bookmakers—those who issued betting slips on which they had no intention of paying out. According to the *Chicago Tribune*, 29 June 1893, 'Many of the "phony" bookmakers in the ring had not enough play to keep them alive.'

The usage of phoney as a noun, meaning 'a false person or thing', came up in the early twentieth century. According to the *Oxford English Dictionary*, its first appearance is in *Six Ex-Tank Tales*—'tank' being short for 'tankard'—a collection of sketches by Clarence Louis Cullen from 1902, which originally appeared in *The New York Sun*: 'If youse tinks f'r a minnit dat youse is goin' t' git away wit' a phony like dat wit' me youse is got hay in y'r hemp, dat's wot.' These tales were supposedly told during 'deliberations of the Harlem Club of Former Alcoholic Degenerates.'

Phoney need not be applied only to con artists and their con games. It can apply to various other things including aspects of language, such as accents. Consider this sentence:

> Vijay picked up his phoney American accent on a weeklong holiday in New York.

Here is another example of the usage of the word—a poem by Vivian Buchan titled 'Phoney Phonetics'. It is about the tricky pronunciation of words:

> One reason why I cannot spell,
> Although I learned the rules quite well
> Is that some words like *coup* and *through*
> Sound just like *threw* and *flue* and *Who*.

3

Pedigree

Have you ever seen a crane standing? If you get out into the countryside often, and you have time on your hands, you might discover that this big bird can spend ages standing—on one foot! You would also observe that its foot has three toes which are splayed out, to allow it to balance.

Apparently, people in fourteenth-century England were fishing around for a term to describe genealogical tables, used to record people's ancestry. That's when they made a connection between the crane's toes and the short vertical lines used to connect one generation to the next in their family trees.

That brings us to the word 'pedigree'. This English word has its origins in Anglo-Norman, a dialect of French, which was the official language in England after William the Conqueror, well, conquered England. He brought with him the language he spoke back home in Normandy, France. Interestingly, though 'pedigree' came into English from this version of French that took hold in old England, it did not exist in modern French till it was exported to France from England in the nineteenth century.

The early version of the word pedigree has its first recorded use in the proceedings of the High Court of Justice in England. The term *pee de gru* was used to describe an ancestral chart. And no, here 'pee' does not mean what you might think it does. In modern French, this would be written as *pied de gru*, literally, 'the foot of the crane'.

By the fifteenth century, the word had passed from

Anglo-Norman into English. It came to refer to not just ancestral charts but the actual bloodlines of people—or animals—in general. Nowadays, 'pedigree' is applied to animals to mean that they are pure-bred. Individuals are said to have refined pedigree if they are descended from so-called 'superior folk': people who have wealth, power or fame.

The word has a cousin that is an English surname: Pettigrew. We find it in the Harry Potter series, for example: Peter Pettigrew is the cowardly villain who betrays the protagonist's parents. According to one theory—in the real world, not the Potter universe—Pettigrew shares its etymology with pedigree. However, it is unclear why or how a surname with the meaning 'a crane's foot' came into use.

Incidentally, pedigree is an important theme in J.K. Rowling's series. It comes with its own invented vocabulary: characters from non-magical bloodlines are known as 'muggles' or 'muggle-born'. And the magicians of non-magical descent are sometimes referred to, derogatorily, as 'mudbloods'.

While the pedigree of the word pedigree is generally accepted to link back to the crane's foot, it is not cast in stone. In fact, some etymologists have claimed the theory does not have a leg to stand on.

That quip was just waiting to be made!

4

Basketball

Necessity is the mother of invention. That's a cliché we've all heard. And the necessity that birthed the invention of basketball was the need for a sport that could be played indoors during winter.

Dr James Naismith was a Canadian physical education teacher at the YMCA International Training School in Springfield, Massachusetts, in the USA. In the winter of 1891, he was asked by Dr Luther Gulick, the director of physical education, to devise an indoor game to help keep the track and field runners in shape. Dr Gulick stipulated that it should be a safe game to play, with minimal contact between players to avoid injuries.

Dr Naismith was given two weeks to come up with this new game. He harked back to his childhood when he and his friends used to play Duck on a Rock, a game that has been around since medieval times. It involves placing a big stone—the duck—on a rock or tree stump. While a defender guards the rock, the other players throw stones at the duck to dislodge it from its place. There's more to the game, of course, but I'll leave it at that for now.

Throwing big stones around was certainly not a safe game, so Dr Naismith decided to use a soccer ball for his new sport. The goal would be to throw the ball into a basket—a half bushel peach basket—nailed high up on the railing of the gym balcony on either end of the court: another way of safeguarding against the injuries that typically happen when two teams clash near the goal zone in sports like American football.

On 21 December 1891, the first-ever game of basketball was played by two teams of nine players each at the YMCA training school. Frank Mahan, one of the players, suggested that the game be called 'Naismith ball' after its inventor. But Naismith laughed and said that that name would kill the game. Then Mahan suggested the name 'basketball'. Naismith replied, 'We have a basket and a ball, and it seems to me that would be a good name for it.' And the name stuck.

The inventor came up with five principles and 13 rules and it was on the basis of these that the game was played. This first game ended 1–0, with the single basket scored by William R. Chase.

YMCA stands for Young Men's Christian Association. Founded in 1845, this global organization believes in serving Christianity by promoting a healthy mind, body and spirit. It was started at a time when the Industrial Revolution drew many young men to the cities, where the only diversions were taverns and brothels. The YMCA—often referred to simply as 'the Y'—wanted to provide a more wholesome alternative to these activities.

The YMCA not only invented basketball but also played a big role in popularizing the game in America and around the world. Duncan Patton, another Canadian who was a part of the Y and also one of the players in that first game played at Springfield, later travelled to India, bringing basketball with him. He served as the acting general secretary for the Calcutta (now Kolkata) YMCA for two years.

Curiously, the peach baskets used in the early days did not have holes in them, so every time a goal was scored the game had to be paused while the janitor got the ball down. Even when holes were introduced in the baskets, they were not made big enough for the ball to fall through and so a stick had to be used to retrieve it. It was only in 1906 that metal hoops with nets replaced the baskets and the ball no longer got stuck. Two years earlier, the soccer ball had been replaced with a ball specifically developed for the game by Spalding at Naismith's request.

While the history of basketball seems clear and straightforward, there is a controversy surrounding its invention. The alternative theory is that the game was actually invented by Lambert G. Will, a director of a YMCA in Herkimer, New York, well before Naismith's famed first game. The main piece of evidence is a photograph of a basketball team in Herkimer from 1892. The intriguing part of it is that the ball in the picture has 1891-92 written on it, implying the team was around in 1891 and therefore could have played basketball before December of that year when Naismith is said to have come up with the game. Of course, Lambert G. Will himself never claimed that he invented basketball—which weakens this theory somewhat. Nevertheless, even today, there are people who insist that Will was the inventor, and that Naismith stole the credit!

The year 1936 was significant for basketball as it debuted at the Berlin Summer Olympics as an official medal sport. The Berlin Olympics were nicknamed Hitler's Olympics because these games were hosted by Nazi Germany. There were many groups and individuals in America and other countries who wanted to boycott these games. But ultimately 49 countries, including the USA, participated, leaving behind Jewish athletes so as not to displease the Nazis—which was a shame.

Coming back to basketball, the final Olympic gold-medal game was played outdoors between the US and Canada on a rain-soaked clay court at the Berlin Tennis Stadium. This was probably the last time ever that international basketball was played outdoors. It was so wet that a journalist commented that it was 'almost like watching a water polo game'.

The Americans defeated the Canadians in this final game. James Naismith, now 74 years old, was present and handed over the medals at the end of the game. He must have been proud that the two countries he called home won the gold and silver. But what must have given him even greater pride was the fact that the game he invented in the previous century was now showered in Olympic glory. Literally and figuratively.

Despite the soggy final and the shadow of Nazism, the 1936 Olympics were a significant moment in the growth of the popularity of basketball in the global arena. And today the number of people who play the game around the world is estimated at over 450 million!

5

Lunatic

What does lunacy have to do with the moon? Plenty, according to long-held popular beliefs. Though there is little or no hard evidence to support it, people are convinced that the moon influences not just the tides in the ocean—which by the way is backed by science—but also the 'tides' in the minds and bodies of human beings. From rheumatism to mental illness to crime, many believe that these spike on full moon nights. Believers in this lunar effect theory offer the explanation that our bodies are 80 per cent water and the pull of the moon on water is undeniable.

Greek philosopher Aristotle and Roman author Pliny both believed that the brain in particular was negatively affected by the moon because of its high liquid content.

Whether a tangible link exists or not, the words 'lunatic' and 'lunacy' are irrevocably connected with the moon. *Luna* means 'moon' in Latin and the word lunatic was coined to refer to people who were insane or mentally unstable. This was based on the belief that these conditions were caused by the moon. The word came into English in the late thirteenth century, either via the French word *lunatique* or directly from the late Latin word *lunaticus*.

The word lunatic was applied legally in English-speaking countries to a person suffering from mental illness. In England the term was eventually replaced by 'mentally ill'. 'Lunatic' was dropped from US federal laws as recently as 2012, when

President Barack Obama signed the legislation into law. However, people continue to use the word informally when they feel someone's behaviour is silly, irrational or extreme. 'He's such a lunatic—writing a book like this!'

A song titled 'Brain Damage' by the rock band Pink Floyd has the line 'I'll see you on the dark side of the moon'. It is from their 1973 album *The Dark Side of the Moon*. Initially titled 'Lunatic', this song was inspired by the mental illness of a band member. It is an example of how popular culture has perpetuated the lunar lunacy belief.

Another line in the song is 'Got to keep the loonies on the path'. 'Loony' is an informal form of the word lunatic that appeared in the mid-nineteenth century. 'Loony bin' was slang for a mental asylum. This terminology is considered offensive today. Even the word asylum has now been replaced by 'hospital'.

The word lunatic has given rise to terms such as 'lunatic fringe'. Lunatic fringe was the name of a hairstyle in the nineteenth century. But the words were later reinterpreted by US president Theodore Roosevelt to refer to members of a group whose views are extreme or fanatical.

'Lunatic soup' is Australian slang for cheap alcohol. The term probably came about because of the way alcohol, cheap or otherwise, affects the mind when consumed in excess.

6

Malaria

'Abracadabra! Is your fever gone?'

If you contracted malaria in the third century—which was long before the word 'malaria' was invented—someone might well have muttered the incantation 'abracadabra' and expected you to get better.

That's because Quintus Serenus Sammonicus, the Roman emperor Caracalla's doctor, had written a medical poem—yes, there is such a thing—asking patients shivering with fever to wear an amulet inscribed with 'abracadabra'. After nine days, you had to take it off and throw it over your shoulder into a stream that ran eastwards.

The word malaria comes to us from *malus aria* in Latin or *mala aria* in Italian. Both mean 'evil air'—the supposed cause of the disease. *Malus* is Latin for 'bad' or 'evil'. *Mala* means the same in Italian. *Aria* is 'air' in both languages.

Malaria is one of the oldest known diseases, though for centuries people were fuzzy about how one got it. They thought it was caused by foul vapours that rose from marshy lands. Hence, 'swamp fever' was another name given to it. Roman soldiers were advised to camp away from bogs to avoid the illness.

The term malaria was probably introduced by Italian physician Francesco Torti (1658–1741) in the eighteenth century.

The foul air theory remained popular till the mid-nineteenth century, only breaking down with the discovery of the malarial parasite in 1847. It was the German doctor Johann Heinrich Meckel who first observed black granules in the blood and spleen of a patient who died of malaria. These were actually malaria parasites.

In 1880, Alphonse Laveran, a French army doctor working in Algeria, properly identified the malarial parasite in the blood of infected patients. He also noted that when treated with quinine, the parasite vanished from the blood.

But it was in India that the story was completed: on 20 August 1897, Sir Ronald Ross, a British doctor working in the subcontinent, discovered that the parasites developed in the *Anopheles* mosquitoes that drank the blood of malaria patients. This won him the 1902 Nobel Prize for Medicine.

Indian tonic water, now known simply as tonic, was invented in India as a preventative drink against malaria. Quinine, the malaria medicine, was bitter, so the British mixed it with soda and sugar to make it palatable. Then they decided to have the tonic with gin, making it an even more agreeable drink. And thus, thanks to malaria, the gin and tonic was invented.

The fact that mosquitoes and other insects cause disease was known in certain parts of the world since ancient times. In the twenty-sixth century BCE, for example, Egyptians ate onions and garlic to ward off mosquitoes. But it was Ross who put the final piece of the puzzle in place and lucked out with the Nobel Prize.

He was so delighted by his achievement that he declared 20 August, the day he made his discovery, Malaria Day—which was later adopted as World Mosquito Day.

7

Sideburn

He gave his name to a gun and a facial hairstyle—though in the latter case, it was back to front!

Ambrose Everett Burnside (1824–81) was a Rhode Island senator and a Union Army general in the American Civil War. By his own admission he was a poor military commander, associated with spectacular defeats in battle. Yet, President Lincoln not only kept him on in the army, but promoted him too.

Perhaps the president was influenced by Burnside's likeable personality, the gun he invented, and his legendary side whiskers. The general is said to have always had a smile on his face and a knack for remembering people's names. The gun he designed and patented—the Burnside carbine—was widely used in the Civil War. Which brings us to his third and, in terms of legacy, most enduring contribution: lending his name to a facial hairstyle.

Sideburns are the strips of hair that come down the sides of a man's face, from the hairline just above the ears to the area just below the ears. When they extend further down towards the chin, they become classified as a beard. Burnside's luxuriant sideburns were connected to his moustache. His chin was clean-shaven.

Before Burnside's sideburns became famous, this section of facial hair was called side whiskers or sideboards. Or, if they were particularly thick, like the general's, they were termed 'mutton chops'—presumably because they resembled said cuts of meat. My sideburns are, of course, far less impressive!

The *Evening Telegraph*, May 1866, has the earliest mention in print of Burnside's hairy legacy: the hairstyle was referred to in it as 'Burnside whiskers'. In the 1870s and '80s, people started calling these whiskers 'burnsides', but by 1887, the syllables were switched and burnside became sideburn, placing 'side' first, perhaps to emphasize the word's association with the sides of the face.

Although sideburns have been around for hundreds of years, they came into their own in the nineteenth century. The trend started with European military men who were inspired by the Hussar regiments, known for their impressive side whiskers.

During World War I, though, soldiers had to be clean-shaven on the sides and chin to wear gas masks. This meant that they could still have moustaches, but beards and sideburns had to go.

A neater version of sideburns became fashionable again, this time among the civilian population, in the mid-twentieth century. These were popularized by the likes of Elvis Presley and James Dean. This time though, in contrast to the earlier military fashion, sideburns became a sign of rebellion.

In the twenty-first century, big sideburns made a comeback with the series of films based on the comic book superhero Wolverine, played on-screen by Australian actor Hugh Jackman.

An alternative theory about the etymology of 'sideburn' is linked to the British soldiers known as 'redcoats'. They used a firearm called the 'flintlock'. When it was fired, gun powder sprayed out of it, causing burns on the side of the face. The soldiers were perhaps encouraged to grow side whiskers as a measure of protection against the burns and also to hide the burn marks. Supporters of this claim find it more plausible than the logic that the syllables of Burnside were flipped to give us the word sideburn.

You decide which story is more convincing.

8

Limerick

A limerick is usually a witty poem of five lines in which the first, second and fifth lines rhyme with each other. And the third and fourth lines, which are shorter than the rest, also rhyme with each other.

Edward Lear (1812–88) is called the father of the limerick because he popularized this form of poetry. Here's a limerick that is attributed to him, though no one's sure if he actually wrote it:

> There was a young lady of Niger
> who smiled as she rode on a tiger;
> They returned from the ride
> with the lady inside,
> and the smile on the face of the tiger.

The Republic of Niger is a country in West Africa. For the purposes of this limerick, Niger is pronounced 'nye-jer'. And the soft 'g' in Niger makes you want to pronounce 'tiger' as 'tijer' for the rhyme, though of course that wouldn't do!

The next limerick was definitely written by Edward Lear:

> There was a Young Lady whose chin
> Resembled the point of a pin:
> So she had it made sharp,
> And purchased a harp,
> And played several tunes with her chin.

Imagine a lady with a pointy chin playing the harp! Hilarious nonsense, isn't it? No wonder Lear called his book of such poems *A Book of Nonsense*. Published in 1846, this book earned him £125, a princely sum for a writer in those days. Since then, a lot of limericks written by various people start with the words 'There was a young lady...' Often, the words that follow are quite bawdy, so I'm not going to share them here.

Another famous writer of limericks was Ogden Nash (1902–71). His sense of humour made him my favourite poet when I was a child. Here's one of my favourite limericks written by Nash:

> A flea and a fly in a flue
> Were imprisoned, so what could they do?
> Said the fly, "let us flee!"
> "Let us fly!" said the flea.
> So they flew through a flaw in the flue.

I love the alliteration—which means the repetition of the same sound at the beginning of words that are placed close to each other, like the 'fl' sound in 'fly', 'flee', 'flea', 'flew', 'flaw' and 'flue' in this limerick.

A flue is the internal shaft of a chimney. Note that this flue is spelt 'f-l-u-e', unlike the disease flu, spelt 'f-l-u', which is short for influenza.

While limericks are generally thought of as humorous poems for adults, they can be nursery rhymes too.

Tommy Thumb's Pretty Songbook was the first collection of English nursery rhymes. It was published in London in 1744. It contained this limerick that I learnt in kindergarten:

> Hickory dickory dock,
> the mouse ran up the clock;

the clock struck one
and down he run;
hickory dickory dock.

The origin of the term 'limerick', first documented in the *Oxford English Dictionary* in 1896, is not clear. It is thought to come from the name of the place called Limerick in Ireland. The earliest published American limerick is from 1902:

There once was a man from Nantucket
Who kept all his cash in a bucket.
But his daughter, named Nan,
Ran away with a man
And as for the bucket, Nantucket.

Nantucket, as mentioned in the first line, is the name of an island in the US. The writer got creative with his wordplay in the last line—where Nantucket is a substitute for the words 'Nan took it'.

It is hard to talk about English without mentioning Shakespeare. Sure enough, he used a limerick as a drinking song in the play *Othello*, which he wrote in 1603. Keep in mind that 'canakin' is the old term for a small can in which drinks are served:

And let me the canakin clink, clink;
And let me the canakin clink
A soldier's a man;
A life's but a span;
Why, then, let a soldier drink.

It seems that limericks were a popular form of drinking song in England and Ireland. Poets used to spar in verse at an Irish pub in Croom, in County Limerick. Here is a repartee between the poets Seán Ó'Tuama (1709–75) and Aindrias MacCraith (1710–93), translated into English by James Clarence Mangan. Ó'Tuama boasted:

> I sell the best Brandy and Sherry
> To make all my customers merry,
> But at times their finances
> Run short as it chances,
> And then I feel very sad, very.

MacCraith's rejoinder:

> O'Tuama! You boast yourself handy
> At selling good ale and bright Brandy,
> But the fact is your liquor
> Makes everyone sicker;
> I tell you this, I, your friend, Andy.

The verse form of the limerick is an old one. Some say it goes back to France in the Middle Ages. But it was Edward Lear who popularized the form with his 1846 book, making him synonymous with limericks—so much so that such verses started being called 'learics' till the word limerick appeared at the end of the nineteenth century. Here's one more of his charming limericks or, rather, learics:

> There was an Old Man with a beard,
> Who said, "It is just as I feared!
> Two Owls and a Hen,
> Four Larks and a Wren,
> Have all built their nests in my beard!"

I think Lear's works justify his reputation as the father of the limerick. As a tribute to him, I have written the following limerick:

Limerick

There was a young writer called Lear
Whose poetry spread far and near
He made people giggle
So much that they'd wriggle
And fall down and bruise their rear.

9
Quarantine

The word 'quarantine' comes from the Italian *quarantino*, derived from *quaranta giorni*, meaning '40 days'. When the word was invented in Italy in the Middle Ages, medical isolation was stipulated to be 40 days long.

This was in the middle of the fourteenth century, when the bubonic plague, or the Black Death, as it was known, infected Europe and ultimately killed off a third of its population. The epidemic started in 1347 in southern Europe and spread to other parts of the continent. By 1359, it had wiped out about one-third of Europe's population—and a significant percentage of Asia's population too.

Rulers took extreme steps to try to stop the plague from spreading, some too gruesome to get into. Ragusa, now known as Dubrovnik and a part of Croatia but then a part of the Venetian Republic, introduced a 30-day isolation period in 1377. It was called *trentino*, derived from the Italian word for the number 30. A *cordon sanitaire* was thrown around the entry point to Ragusa. New arrivals by ship had to spend a month within this Lakshman Rekha to be allowed access to the rest of the city. Conversely, inhabitants of Ragusa were barred from this zone. Those who broke the rule were not allowed to leave for a month.

The measure seemed beneficial and was gradually adopted by other Mediterranean cities. Along the way, the period of isolation increased by 10 days, and 'trentino' became 'quarantino'. It is from the latter word that we get the English 'quarantine'.

Why the period was extended from 30 to 40 days is not known. Some believe that it was simply because the longer duration was found more effective in curbing infection. Others think that it could have been based on the Greek medical belief in 'critical days'—that it took 40 days for an infection to develop in a person who has been exposed to a disease. Another explanation is that it was influenced by the Biblical associations with 40 days—the period for which Lent, a prescribed duration for spiritual purification, is observed. It is also the duration of the great flood, of Moses' stay on Mt Sinai, and of Jesus's wanderings in the wilderness.

The practice of quarantining, though not the term itself, predates the plague. Leprosy patients have been isolated for centuries to prevent the spread of the disease. An early mention of it is in Leviticus, the third book of the Old Testament, written in the seventh century BCE or earlier.

Quarantining can sometimes lead to ethical concerns, such as in the case of Typhoid Mary. Mary Mallon, an Irish cook in the United States, was an asymptomatic carrier of typhoid. Wherever she worked, there were outbreaks of typhoid. Eventually, the infections were linked to her and she was nicknamed Typhoid Mary. Mary ended up spending three decades of her life in forced isolation. If you thought 40 days was too long, imagine being locked up for life! Today, the Siracusa Principles are used as guidelines for balancing human rights considerations with extreme measures to prevent dread diseases from spreading.

Quarantines continue to be observed around the world. But they are no longer required to be followed for a period of 40 days. A quarantine today lasts as long as medical science deems necessary to render patients infection-free.

The most significant use of quarantines in recent times, of course, occurred during the Covid-19 pandemic.

10

Deadline

I was supposed to finish writing this book earlier, but I missed my deadline. Luckily, I did not have to pay the kind of penalty for overshooting the time limit that the original meaning of 'deadline' suggests.

The word itself contains a clue as to its old meaning. Two clues, actually: 'dead' and 'line'. It was a line in a prison yard. If you crossed it, you were shot dead. Such was the violent beginning of this word.

The term arose during the American Civil War, most likely at a prison camp in Andersonville, Georgia, which was notorious for the hellish conditions under which it kept its prisoners. The Civil War was fought from 1861 to 1865 between the northern US states that made up the Union and the southern US states that had broken away to form the Confederacy. The prisoners at this camp were northerners—aka Yankees—who had been captured by the Confederates of the south.

The earliest reference to 'deadline' in this sense has been found in the diary of William Williston Heartsill, a prisoner, dated March 1863:

> The guard lines are drawn in; making our play grounds much smaller and cutting us off from our best well of water, this is done for no other purpose under the sun but to interfere with our only enjoyment and to grind us to the lowest depth of subjugation. The the [sic] two sutler

stores are moved inside the dead-line, all right Mr Lynch we may meet you when we will have "the say" on you.

You get a better sense of its violent meaning from this description in an 1864 report by the United States Sanitary Commission:

> Twenty feet inside and parallel to the fence is a light railing, forming the "dead line," beyond which the projection of a foot or finger is sure to bring the deadly bullet of the sentinel...
> [...] One poor fellow [...] was trying to wash his face near the "dead line" railing, when he slipped on the clayey bottom, and fell with his head just outside the fatal border. We shouted to him, but it was too late...

At some point in the nineteenth century, the word deadline started being used in printing presses in a different sense (though still not the current one). There was a safe zone in which you had to set the type for printing. If you set it outside this zone, it did not get printed; it was 'dead'. The line demarcating this zone was known as a deadline.

Today, a deadline is simply a time limit for completing something—usually not a life-or-death situation. Often, you can even get an extension on the time limit. I, for example, was not shot dead for missing the original deadline for this book, so here you are, reading it!

11
Boycott

The Irish and the Indians have a shared history of rising up against British subjugation, and Indian freedom fighters took inspiration from the successes of the Irish people.

In 1905, the British divided the state of Bengal into two—East and West Bengal. The division was along communal lines. The intent was to curb the growing power of Bengal by fostering disunity—the famous 'divide and rule' policy of the British Raj.

The Bengali intelligentsia resented this move and passed a boycott resolution in the Calcutta City Hall (now Kolkata Town Hall) on 7 August 1905.

Now what does the word 'boycott' mean exactly? Well, the meaning has evolved over time. But let me try to give you a comprehensive definition which includes its different aspects. To 'boycott' means to withdraw from commercial or social relations with a country, organization or person as a means of protest or punishment. It is usually done for social, political, moral or environmental reasons. The purpose is to change the objectionable behaviour of the target by expressing moral outrage or inflicting economic loss.

I know—that was quite a mouthful. But let's go back to the Bengal boycott of 1905 to get a better sense of the concept. That boycott took the form of rejecting British goods like cloth, sugar and salt. It was extended to staying away from all colonial government institutions like schools, colleges, courts and legislative councils. This protest spread from Calcutta to the rest of the country and became the Swadeshi Movement, which played a key role in the Indian struggle for independence.

While this boycott movement was one of the earliest the world saw, the first boycott took place in Ireland 25 years earlier. That was actually where the word boycott was born.

It was 1880. After a year of bad harvests, Lord Erne, an absentee landlord, decided to be 'generous' and offer his tenants a 10 per cent discount on their rent. The tenants asked for a bigger reduction to help them make ends meet, but the ruthless landlord decided to evict these tenants rather than accept their demand. And for this job he sent his land agent, Captain Charles Boycott.

Aha! So is that where the word came from? Yes! Here is the rest of the story: shortly before this incident, Charles Stewart Parnell, leader of the Irish National Land League, gave a speech encouraging the social ostracism of new tenants who took the places of evicted tenants. Now Captain Boycott had to find other tenants or seasonal workers to harvest the crops. But it was understood by the locals that those who took the place of the evicted tenants would be socially shunned. So, nobody came forward. Finally, Boycott had to bring in 50 men from other areas to harvest the crop. He arranged for a regiment of the 19th Royal Hussars and more than 1,000 men of the Royal Irish Constabulary to protect the harvesters, because it was beyond Boycott's understanding that this was a non-violent protest. The exercise ended up costing the British government more than £10,000 to harvest crops worth just about £500.

Boycott himself was socially isolated not only by his employees but also by others in the community. His household help abandoned him. Local businessmen stopped trading with him. Shops refused to serve him. Even the postman stopped delivering his mail.

Boycott rapidly became a household name as first the British and then the international press picked up the story. James Redpath of the *New-York Tribune* was the first overseas reporter to write about the boycott. The first documented usage of the word in its figurative sense is found in the 22 January 1881 edition of *The Spectator*: 'Dame Nature arose.... She "Boycotted" London from Kew to Mile End.'

And thus, a name became a word almost overnight. Some new words die out fast. But this one kept living on, though the context and manner of its use evolved. It often takes the form of consumer activism today—via social media—where people are discouraged from buying branded products from companies that degrade the environment, use child labour, or practise discrimination based on race, gender, religion or sexual orientation.

There is even an app for it. It scans the barcode on a product and tells you whether its parent company sources genetically modified ingredients, has unacceptable carbon emissions, or conducts cruel animal testing. If the practices of the company do not conform to your values, you simply boycott the brand.

12

Gossip

Erma Bombeck, the American humorist, once said, 'Some say our national pastime is baseball. Not me. It's gossip.' Richard Steele, the Irish writer, said, 'Fire and swords are slow engines of destruction, compared to the tongue of a Gossip.' From these two quotes we can conclude that gossip is both harmful and rampant!

Ironically, Richard Steele founded a famous magazine called *Tatler* in the early eighteenth century, which covered the lifestyles of the rich and fashionable who, as we know, are always surrounded by gossip. And the name 'Tatler' seems like a variation on the word 'tattler', a synonym for 'gossip'.

Gossip means talk or reports about a person's life—often their private life—which may be malicious or entirely untrue. To talk in this manner is to gossip, the verb form of the word. A person who gossips is also called a gossip, a tattler or a gossipmonger—one who spreads rumours about others.

The word gossip has travelled a long distance from its origin—the Old English noun 'godsibb', recorded around the year 1014. That's over a thousand years ago! This word was made up of 'god' and 'sibb', the latter meaning 'akin to' or 'related to'. In a similar way, the word 'sibling', composed of 'sib(b)' and the suffix '-ling', means 'one who is of kin to another'—a brother or sister. The 'god' part of the word godsibb is connected to the 'god' in godfather or godmother—someone who acts as a sponsor at a Christian baptism. So, originally, 'gossip' referred to a godfather or godmother, a person who formed a close spiritual bond with not just the baptized child, but also its parents and the other godparent.

From the sense of the bond between parents and godparents, the word gossip came to refer to a friend. The Irish author Henry Brooke used the word in this sense in his book *The Fool of Quality; or, the History of Henry Earl of Moreland*, published in five volumes from 1765 to 1770. 'Walter Warmhouse,' he wrote, 'a substantial farmer in Essex, was advised, by serjeant Craw, that he had an unquestionable right to a certain tenement in the possession of Barnaby Boniface, his next neighbour and gossip...'

'Gossip' was also commonly used to refer to a woman's female friends invited to be present at a birth. Thomas Fuller, the Church of England clergyman, wrote in *The History of the Worthies of England* (1662): 'It was fashionable for the Clergy [...] to have their Surnames [...] superadded to those given at the Font, from the places of their Nativity, and therefore they are as good evidence to prove where they were born, as if we had the deposition of the Midwife, and all the Gossips present at their Mothers labours.'

Giving birth was a social event for women. The pregnant woman's female relatives and neighbours would gather for it. Perhaps it is because they would indulge in idle conversation during these events that gossip came to mean 'to talk of others'. However, there is no evidence to suggest that women have a monopoly on gossip in the current sense. Men probably indulge in it just as much.

Gossip flows in organizations through informal networks known as 'the grapevine'. You know, like in the 1960s superhit song 'I Heard It through the Grapevine'. The lyrics go:

> Don'tcha know that I
> Heard it through the grapevine
> Not much longer would you be mine
> Oh I heard it through the grapevine
> Oh I'm just about to lose my mind

The song highlights the pain of a person who has heard through gossip that he or she is going to get dumped.

The song was written for Motown Records and the first recording of it, released in 1967, was by the group Gladys Knight & the Pips. It became the biggest-selling Motown Records single released until then. It has been performed by various other musicians. The version I like the most was sung by Marvin Gaye. Released in 1968, it surpassed the Gladys Knight & the Pips version and became for a time the biggest hit single of the Motown label.

Coming back to the corporate world, managers sometimes find it more convenient to gather information through the grapevine rather than more formal channels. But whether it be at the workplace or in society at large, this so-called information or gossip may be a deliberate distortion of the facts designed to harm certain individuals. It's a terrible thing to be a victim of it.

Gossip was and is used as a way of pressurizing people to conform to socially acceptable behaviour. This function of it is used by some to legitimize it. Will Rogers (1879–1935), the American actor and social commentator, wrote, 'Live in such a way that you would not be ashamed to sell your parrot to the town gossip.' This was his witty way of explaining the social function of gossip.

But there is a thin line between gossiping about others to 'keep them in line' and seriously harming their reputation with distorted accounts of their private life. Many religions actually disapprove of this sort of talk. In Islam, for example, backbiting is likened to eating the flesh of one's dead brother. This underlines the worst aspect of gossip—the victim does not get a chance to defend themselves against it, just as the dead cannot defend themselves against their flesh being eaten.

Today, gossip can spread to millions in an instant through social media. Politicians and celebrities are particularly easy targets. But they are not the only ones. In student communities, cyber-gossip often escalates to cyber-bullying, which can be traumatic for the victim. This is why it behoves each one of us to verify information before sharing it—knowing that it has the power to ruin careers and shatter self-esteem. With that great power comes great responsibility!

Economist Walter Block has argued that blackmailers are ethically superior to gossips because they give the victims the option of not disclosing damaging information about them in exchange for money. The victim of gossip is not given this choice. It is perhaps an interesting way of underlining just how low on the scale of righteousness gossiping is—it makes blackmailing look comparatively ethical!

13

Braille

Can you read with your hands? Sounds unfeasible? Well, that is how blind people read: a feat that is possible because of an accident a three-year-old child had while playing, two centuries ago in France.

The child was Louis Braille (1809–52). His father was a leather artisan. One day, Louis was playing in his father's workshop with an awl, a small pointed tool used for punching holes in leather. He accidentally jabbed himself in the eye with it. The eye got infected and the infection spread to the other eye as well. Despite the doctor's best efforts, Louis became completely blind. Not understanding what had happened to him, little Louis would keep asking why it was so dark all the time.

Luckily for Louis, his parents sent him to one of the world's first schools for the blind, the Royal Institute for Blind Youth in Paris. Its founder had devised a system of raised letters using the normal English alphabet, which the children could trace with their fingers, and that is how Louis first learned to read. But the books were difficult to make, costly, cumbersome and fragile. So much so that initially there were only three such books in the school.

One day Louis Braille learned of a system called night writing. It was devised by Captain Charles Barbier of Napoleon Bonaparte's French army. Soldiers used to read combat messages after dark using lamps, which made them easy targets for the enemy. Night writing, which could be read by the touch of your fingers, solved this problem. Over time, Braille refined night writing to create what we know today as braille.

When he was only 15, Louis had already created a working model of braille—a system that used six raised dots in different patterns to recreate the alphabet. Ironically, Louis used the awl, the same instrument that blinded him, to develop his raised-dot communication system.

Louis Braille stayed on at the institute where he studied for most of his life, becoming a professor of history and mathematics there. But braille was not adopted at the very place he taught until two years after his death. In fact, during his lifetime, the school authorities insisted on using the old system. They were actively against braille. After Louis passed away, the students pressurized the school into implementing the far superior braille system.

Over the next few decades, braille spread throughout the world as the standard system of writing and reading for the blind, which can be used for any number of languages. By the mid-nineteenth century, the French surname Braille had become the English word braille, used to denote the system that Louis invented while still a mere schoolboy.

14

Sinister

If your day is not going well, you might wonder whether you woke up on the wrong side of the bed—which is what the left side of the bed has traditionally been thought of as. The right side of the bed, on the other hand, is considered the *right* side—the good, correct and auspicious side.

In many cultures, there is a historical bias against the left-hand side. And that is why the word 'sinister', derived from the Latin word for 'left', has come to mean what it does in English—'something or someone that gives you the impression that evil might happen'. The word 'left' itself betrays a bias, too, coming as it does from the old English word 'lyft', which meant 'weak'. The bias is present in other languages as well: *gauche*, the French word for left, means 'awkward'.

The prejudice carries into the real world: from school desks to scissors to doorknobs, things are designed for the right-handed majority.

Perhaps your parents or teachers pressurized you to switch to the right hand which didn't come naturally to you. The next time someone scoffs at you for being left-handed, tell them that Bill Clinton, Barack Obama, Ratan Tata, Amitabh Bachchan and Mother Teresa are just some of the personalities who share this unique trait with you!

Also, International Lefthanders Day, observed on 13 August, seeks to acknowledge 'lefties' in a world that's dominated by right-handed individuals.

Coming back to the word 'sinister'. Its etymology can be traced to the Latin word *sinistra*. It started being used in English in its evil sense by the fifteenth century. In Latin, the word was used in the context of augury—the practice of interpreting the flight of birds as good or bad omens.

The act of interpretation was known as 'taking the auspices'. If the birds flew to the right, it was considered 'auspicious', and to the left, 'inauspicious'. That's where the ominous connotation of sinister comes from.

The opposite of sinister in Latin is *dexter*, meaning 'right-handed' or 'on the right-hand side'. In a broader sense, it means 'skilful' or 'favourable'. You may know this word from the famous book or TV series *Dexter*. The word 'dextrous' is derived from dexter, showing the positive predisposition to the right-hand side.

The word 'ambidextrous' also comes, in part, from the same root. While it means 'the ability to use both hands equally well', its literal Latin meaning is 'having two right hands'. So biased were people against the left hand that they had to think of it as another right hand if it could be used well! The feet do not fare much better: if you cannot dance, you are said to have two left feet.

'Sinister' and 'dexter' have been used in heraldry as well. The right or dexter half of the shield had greater honour. The shields of illegitimate children were marked by a 'bar sinister'. In the Great Seal of the United States, the eagle holds an olive branch in its dexter talon and arrows in its sinister talon—an intention of peace on the right, with a threat of war on the sinister side!

Politics is one area in which 'left' does not have a negative meaning—except to those who are from the political right. These political terms arose during the French Revolution: in the National Assembly, supporters of the king sat to the right of the president, and supporters of the revolution sat to his left. This seating arrangement led to terminology such as 'leftist' and 'left-wing'.

By and large, though, the left hand and the words associated with it in various languages occupy a spectrum of meaning that ranges from the mildly negative 'awkward' to the decidedly unpleasant 'sinister'. In most cases, 'right' is considered right and 'left', wrong—sinister indeed for the left-handed.

15
Thug / Loot / Dacoit

Is it a crime to take words from another language and put them in yours? I don't think so. But if it were, then the English would be behind bars! Here are just three of the many words that the English 'took' from India:

thug

'Thug' comes from the Indian word *thag*—which means 'deceiver' or 'swindler'. Thags were highway robbers who would disguise themselves as travellers. They would befriend other travellers and strangle them with handkerchiefs when they were least expecting it and then proceed to loot them.

But first let's look at the American version of thug. Rapper Tupac gave the word a whole new meaning with his 'thug life' tattoo. According to him, it was an acronym for 'The Hate U Give Little Infants F***s Everybody', implying that people turn to crime because of the way they were treated by society when they were young.

loot

'Loot' is another word the British, literally, looted from India. Originating from a similar word in Hindi, it first appears in an eighteenth-century book called *Indian Vocabulary*, which was connected to the impeachment of Warren Hastings, governor-general of Bengal. Accused of looting the place instead of governing it, he was later acquitted. It's ironic that Hastings was punished for plundering and looting, given that history shows us that these activities became a hallmark of the Raj.

dacoit

Dacoits are gangs of armed robbers. And dacoity is defined by the Indian penal code as an armed robbery committed by no less than five people! The words came into English from the Indian words *dakait* and *dakaity*.

By the mid-1800s, 'dacoit' and 'dacoity' had become common Anglo-Indian words, appearing in colonial glossaries and legal codes. The East India Company set up a dedicated Thuggee and Dacoity Department in 1830 with the mission of suppressing armed robbery and 'thuggee'—the cult of highway stranglers. At the same time, tales of dacoits began permeating colonial literature and reports. For instance, Rudyard Kipling wrote of British soldiers chasing Burmese dacoits in his story 'The Taking of Lungtungpen'.

Throughout the late colonial period, various incidents and figures exemplified what dacoit and dacoity meant, helping cement the words in popular imagination. One notorious case was the Kakori Train Dacoity of 1925, when a band of Indian revolutionaries led by Ram Prasad Bismil and Ashfaqullah Khan held up a train carrying government funds. The British, eager to downplay this act of anticolonial heroism, treated it as a simple criminal dacoity. According to *The Economic Times* article 'How 1925 Kakori Train Dacoity Led India to a Revolutionary Path for Independence', it was a 'small incident of dacoity at a sleepy railway station' that nonetheless 'shook the might of [the] British empire'. Of course, the revolutionaries—labelled as common dacoits—were hanged.

The Chambal region was once so notorious for dacoits that it entered Indian lore and cinema. Dacoits like Gabbar Singh

Gujjar and Man Singh terrorized the countryside in the 1940s and '50s. Gabbar Singh's story inspired the classic Hindi film *Sholay* (1975).

So, there you have it. Dacoit. Loot. Thug. Three words looted from India.

16

Cannibal / Avocado / Chilli

Geography was not Italian explorer Christopher Columbus's strong suit. He sailed to America and thought he had 'discovered' India. Thanks to him, Europeans started calling the indigenous people of the Americas 'Indians'. He also made the mistake of thinking he 'discovered' the place. Since people were already living there for centuries, it would be safe to say *they* discovered it. Not just Columbus but all Europeans ignored the facts and wholeheartedly embraced these mistakes as the truth.

Thanks to the colonization that followed these geographical and historical blunders, the Indians of the Americas lost out on a lot of things. The English language, on the other hand, gained words from them. Here are three examples:

cannibal

This word comes from another mistake of Columbus's.

He heard from the native Taíno people of the Caribbean (a subgroup of the Arawak family of indigenous people) that there were fearsome islanders called Caniba (or Caribes) who raided their villages. The Taíno showed Columbus scars and marks of wounds on their bodies and explained through signs that people from other nearby islands would attack and try to capture them. According to Columbus's diary, the Taíno spoke in awed fear of these invaders.

Although Columbus never personally caught the Canibas in an act of cannibalism, he interpreted whatever he understood of the Taíno people's testimony as proof that they were 'cannibals'. Drawing on medieval travel myths and Greco-Roman legends, Columbus even described these island raiders as mythical beings with 'snouts of dogs, who ate men', according to William Keegan, curator of anthropology at the Florida Museum of Natural History.

It was convenient for Spanish authorities to believe the Caribbean people to be cannibals because it justified enslaving them. And thus, myth became officially established as 'the truth'. But, till date, little or no evidence has been found to back the claims of widespread cannibalism among the Caniba.

avocado

The Aztecs thought these fruits looked like testicles and hence coined the word *āhuacatl* for them. 'Āhuacatl' means 'testicle' in their native language Nahuatl. This gave rise to the Spanish word *aguacate*, which became 'avocado' in English.

chilli

'Chilli' is another word from the Nahuatl language of the Aztecs. Did you know that not just the word, but the chilli itself originated in the Americas? It did not exist anywhere else in the world. Not even in India! But can you imagine Indian food without it today? Well, that's one thing you can thank Columbus for.

17

Bluetooth / Ritzy / Sandwich / Silhouette

Here are four names that became words:

Bluetooth

'Bluetooth'—we all sort of know what it means. It's the wireless technology that connects mobile phones with computers and other electronic devices. But why is it called Bluetooth? Does it have something to do with a rotten old tooth that's turned blue?

Apparently, it does. In fact, the original Bluetooth is more than a thousand years old! The Danish king Harald 'Bluetooth' Gormsson was famous for two things. One, he united Demark and Norway in the tenth century. And two, he had a dead tooth with a grey-blue colour that earned him the nickname Bluetooth.

In the 1990s, when companies like Intel, Ericsson and Nokia met to standardize the technology, Jim Kardash of Intel suggested the codename Bluetooth because it was a technology that was going to unite the PC and cellular industries, the way the original 'Bluetooth' had united Scandinavia. The codename was to be replaced at the time of launch with a snazzier name by the marketing people in these multinationals. PAN (Personal Area Networking) and RadioWire were the two front runners, but by the date of the launch of the technology, neither name had been cleared by 'legal'. Hence, Bluetooth remained the only viable option. The Bluetooth logo is a combination of the letters 'H' and 'B', the initials of Harald Bluetooth, written in runes, the ancient letters used by the Vikings, the Scandinavian seafaring pirates and traders.

As it turned out, the name Bluetooth became an overnight sensation and has remained unchanged since the time it was first launched in 1999.

ritzy

'Ritzy' refers to something expensive, stylish or fancy.

It's derived from the name of César Ritz, a Swiss waiter in Paris, who gained enough refinement and confidence to transform himself into a hotelier.

Ritz went on to buy and open several hotels with the motto 'The customer is always right'. In 1896, he formed the Ritz Hotel syndicate and opened what would become Hôtel Ritz of Paris. His success led him to be known as the 'king of hoteliers, and hotelier to kings'.

sandwich

The origins of the sandwich, as we know it, can be traced back to a story involving John Montagu, the 4th Earl of Sandwich. He didn't really 'invent' the sandwich, but he certainly seems to have popularized it.

It is said that in 1762, he asked for meat to be served to him between slices of bread, so he could hold his meal in one hand and continue to gamble with the other.

Soon, people started ordering 'the same as Sandwich', and the name stuck!

The earls of Sandwich get their title from a place called Sandwich in Kent, England. Oddly enough, they don't live there.

Edward Montagu, the 1st Earl, was supposed to take the title 'the Earl of Portsmouth'. But because he was commanding a fleet that was anchored off Sandwich, he changed it.

The 11th Earl of Sandwich—the father of the current (12th) Earl of Sandwich—was a direct descendant of the 4th Earl, John Montagu, who was also his namesake. Taking advantage of his title and the story associated with it, he launched a chain of sandwich restaurants called Earl of Sandwich.

By the way, if you do meet the current earl, the correct way to address him would be Lord Sandwich. British titles are so confusing!

silhouette

Your silhouette is your shape viewed against light—a dark solid shape with none of the inside details. This word comes from the name of Étienne de Silhouette, a French finance minister in the eighteenth century. War-ravaged France was in a financial crisis, so he imposed severe economic restrictions, especially on the wealthy. In retaliation, they started to refer to anything cheaply made as silhouettes. Now, before photography was invented, cut-out black profiles of people were the cheapest way to record a person's appearance. So these profiles came to be called silhouettes—cheap substitutes for the portraits you could no longer afford to get painted!

18
Safari / Orange / Algebra

You may be surprised to know that Arabic is a big contributor to English vocabulary. Everyday words like 'cotton', 'coffee' and 'giraffe' are Arabic in origin. Some of these words undertook interesting journeys to become a part of the English language.

safari

'Safari', for example, was borrowed in the 1850s from the Swahili word *safari*, meaning 'journey' or 'expedition', which in turn came from the Arabic *safar*, meaning 'journey' or 'tour'. This word travelled to India as well via Urdu—which is why you and I are quite familiar with the word.

orange

Another Arabic word, *naranj*, entered various European languages and morphed into the English word 'orange'. Along the way it gave rise to words like *naranja* in Spanish, which means the same thing. It's spelt with a 'j' but the Spaniards pronounce 'j' like 'hha', hence it's pronounced 'naranhha'. You can positively hear the Arabic influence in the 'hha'. Not surprising, given that the Arabs ruled Spain for a thousand years.

This word sounds familiar to Indians too—because it is linked to the Hindi word *narangi*, among others. So, did we get this word from Arabic, like we got 'safar'? Nope. This safari was in the opposite direction.

It started out as a similar sounding word in a Dravidian

language—possibly the Tamil *naaram*, the Telugu *naarimja*, or the Malayalam *naaranga*—which entered Sanskrit as *naarangah*, meaning 'orange-tree', and from there into Persian as *naarang* and then Arabic as *naaranj*. And then, eventually, via a couple of other European languages, into English. Phew! What a journey. Made me thirsty for a glass of—what else—orange juice!

Before English got the word orange for the fruit and the colour, the orange colour was described as yellow-red. The other distinction that the word orange enjoys is that it is one of a number of English words like 'purple', 'silver', 'month' and 'dangerous' that have no rhyme!

algebra

When you studied algebra in school, did you at times feel like there was no rhyme or reason to those quadratic equations? Well, you have Arabic to blame for that too. The word 'algebra' comes from the long and complicated title of an Arabic book on mathematics written by Persian polymath Muhammad ibn Musa al-Khwarizmi around 820 CE. The title of the book is *Kitab al-Mukhtasar fi Hisab al-Jabr w'al-Muqabala*—'The Compendious Book on Calculation by Completion and Balancing'. The Latin translation of this book was the main maths textbook in European universities right up to the sixteenth century. And *al-jabr* became 'algebra' during that time.

It was also during this time that Roman numerals (I, II, III, IV...) were replaced with what is known as the Hindu–Arabic numeral system (0, 1, 2, 3, 4...).

19

Machiavellian

I have never taken the MACH-IV test—but if I did, I would wish to get low marks on it. This personality survey was devised by psychologists to test how 'Machiavellian' you are—a psychological trait characterized by manipulativeness, emotional coldness and an absence of morality. This psychological profile is named after a Renaissance-era Italian gentleman called Niccolò Machiavelli.

Considered the father of political science, he was a politician, diplomat, historian, philosopher and writer. Even today, his book *The Prince* is likely to be on the reading list of every political science student and the bookshelf of every statesman. But, because the advice he gave to princes and politicians supposedly required a deceitful and callous mindset to carry out, his surname turned into an adjective for such undesirable traits.

Perhaps he has been given a worse rap than he deserves, though. Some of his advice seems reasonable to me. If I were a political leader—which I am clearly not cut out to be—I would probably follow his counsel.

'The first method for estimating the intelligence of a ruler is to look at the men he has around him,' he wrote. I agree. After all, just being in the position of the leader does not automatically mean that a person is up to the task.

As Machiavelli put it, 'It is not titles that honour men, but men that honour titles.' In other words, you have to show results to be respected.

Machiavelli tempered his pragmatism with empathy: 'The best fortress is to be found in the love of the people, for although you may have fortresses, they will not save you if you are hated by the people.'

Shakespeare said, 'The quality of mercy is not strained'—meaning that one should be generous with it. But Machiavelli advised princes to dole it out with prudence. Too much mercy could backfire on you, so be cruel when necessary to nip a potential menace in the bud—advice that seems a bit, well, Machiavellian.

But it worked for politicians like Cesare Borgia, the illegitimate son of Pope Alexander VI, whose cruelty helped him quell rebellions. Borgia was an inspiration for Machiavelli's theories.

The word 'Machiavellian' makes one of its earliest English appearances in Thomas Nashe's 1592 work *Pierce Penniless His Supplication to the Devil*. In Randle Cotgrave's 1611 work *A Dictionarie of the French and English Tongues*, Machiavellianism (though spelt slightly differently) is defined as 'subtle policy, cunning roguery'.

Ultimately, Machiavelli's approach was realist, and this led him to ignore the moral implications of his recommendations.

Pragmatic or evil, however you want to look at it, his advice has value—the reason why he is still followed today by leaders, both in the political and corporate worlds.

As Machiavelli himself said, 'Since my intention is to say something that will prove of practical use to the inquirer, I have thought it proper to represent things as they are in real truth, rather than as they are imagined.'

Let us judge him accordingly.

20

Indigo

Indigo is one of the oldest dyes on Earth. It was probably invented during the bronze age in the Indus Valley Civilization (3300–1300 BCE). I remember studying about this civilization in history class and feeling proud that 'our' civilization was so rich and ancient. One of the oldest in the world and certainly the largest known, its estimated population was 5,000,000 people. When one of its cities, Rojdi (in modern-day Gujarat), was excavated, archaeologists found seeds belonging to the *Indigofera* plant family, from which indigo dye is made. Remnants of cloth dyed blue from 1750 BCE were found in another centre of this civilization, Mohenjo-daro, located in modern-day Larkana, in Sindh, Pakistan. It is believed that the blue stripes on Egyptian linen mummy cloths were also dyed with indigo.

Fifty or more varieties of *Indigofera* grow in India. *Indigofera tinctoria* is the kind most popularly used to produce indigo. For centuries, these plants have been processed into small cakes of pigment and exported. Indigo reached Europe through the traditional trade route known as the Silk Road. It was bought by the ancient Greeks and Romans (300 BCE–400 CE) as a luxury item.

The Greeks named the dye *indikon*, meaning 'from India'. This passed into Latin as *indicum* or *indico* and came into English as 'indigo' through the old Portuguese word *endego*.

Roman naturalist Pliny the Elder recorded the fact that indigo came to Europe from India in his encyclopaedia *Naturalis*

Historia. Europeans believed that indigo was of mineral origin till the late thirteenth century, when Marco Polo observed during his travels in the East that it was extracted from plants.

Because of its compact form, durability and high price, indigo was a valuable trade item and came to be known as 'blue gold'. When Vasco da Gama discovered a sea route between Europe and India, it became easier for Europeans to import indigo. Until then, a similar dye made from the woad plant was common in Europe. But with larger amounts of indigo being produced in India and exported by ship, its price fell and it became the most commonly used dye in Europe by the end of the seventeenth century.

Inspired by the dye, the name indigo has been given to a deep, rich colour close to the primary colour blue. It is interesting to note that this colour is not exactly the same as the colour that one would obtain from the dye. In his work in the field of optics, English physicist Isaac Newton (1642–1727) described indigo as one of the seven basic colours. In his famous experiments, he produced a band of rainbow colours on the wall by allowing sunlight to pass through a prism. While he acknowledged that the band of colours contained 'an indefinite variety of intermediate gradations', he divided it into seven basic colours—red, yellow, green, blue, violet-purple, orange and indigo.

British planters had a monopoly over indigo cultivation in eighteenth- and nineteenth-century India. They forced farmers to grow indigo instead of food crops and then sell it to them at unprofitable rates so as to maximize their profits. Decades of cruel conditions provoked the Indigo Rebellion of Bengal in 1859–60. In this largely peaceful revolt, the farmers refused to grow indigo and were brutally suppressed by the British. Dinabandhu Mitra's play *Nil Darpan* vividly described the plight of the farmers. The Bengali intelligentsia and European missionaries backed the revolt. Reverend James Long translated the play into English under the title *The Mirror of Indigo*. The planters, the villains in the play, sued him and the missionary had to pay a fine of ₹1,000, a large sum in that day, and spend a month in jail.

Adolf von Baeyer, a German chemist, produced synthetic indigo in 1897. This was easier and cheaper to manufacture and quickly superseded natural indigo. Baeyer won the Nobel Prize in Chemistry in 1905 for his work on dyes, including indigo. While 19,000 tonnes of natural indigo were produced till the advent of the synthetic version, its production rapidly dwindled to about 1,000 tonnes by 1914. The ubiquity of synthetic indigo-dyed yarn, on the other hand, is evidenced by the so-called blue jeans that most of us have in our closet.

Environmental concerns have led to a renewed interest in natural indigo today. The manufacture of synthetic indigo dye from petrochemicals produces hazardous wastes. While natural indigo is more expensive than the synthetic variety, we should keep in mind that the price we pay for this dye named after India protects the life of our planet and the livelihood of our farmers.

21

Lemon

When life gives you lemons, you make lemonade. This proverb means that when things go sour, adopt a can-do attitude and make the best of what you have. One of the earliest appearances of a version of this saying was in the 1915 obituary of American dwarf actor Marshall Pinckney Wilder. The obituarist, Elbert Hubbard, wrote: 'He picked up the lemons that Fate had sent him and started a lemonade stand.'

Of course, when life gives me lemons, I study their etymology.

The lemon tree is a species of small evergreen trees known as *Citrus limon* (L.) Osbeck. Its fruits are oval, yellow and sour. The tree is native to India, so it would be logical if the word too originated in this country. However, things are rarely that simple, and there are multiple theories about its etymology.

It is believed that the fruits were taken home to the Levant from India by Arabs in the ninth or tenth centuries. And from there, they spread to Europe. The Arabic and Persian words for the fruit, *laimun* and *limun* respectively, became *limone* in Italian or Provençal (the language of Provence, Southern France). 'Limone' passed into Old French as *limon*, meaning 'citrus fruit', and thence to English around the year 1400 as 'lymon'. This part of the journey of the word is reasonably clear, but the route that led to it is not. Some say the origin of the Arabic and Persian words for lemon is Austronesian—a family of languages spoken in the area between the Pacific Islands in the east and Madagascar in the west. Specifically, the Balinese word for lemon, *limo*, or the Malay *limaw*, meaning 'citrus fruit' or 'lime', are suggested as the forebears of the word lemon.

The Persian word 'limun' is considered by some scholars to have come from the Sanskrit word *nimbu*. Others say that the Sanskrit word goes further back, to Tamil. Lemons, or citrus fruits, are called *elimicham pazham* in Tamil. 'Pazham' means 'fruit'. 'Elimicham' can be broken down into *eli + micham*. 'Eli' means 'rat' and 'micham' is 'leftovers'. The term is based on the fact that rats eat other fruits but will not touch lemons. Apparently, *elimichi*, a variant form of elimicham, became *limma* and *nimma* in Telugu. This entered Sanskrit as 'nimbu'.

Those who dispute the Indian origin of the word point out that in India, the word lemon is used to refer to what is actually a lime. This is true. In Bengali, for example, the word *lebu*—derived from the Sanskrit nimbu—when used on its own denotes either a lime or a lemon. A *kamala lebu* is an orange. A *musambi lebu* is a sweet lime or sweet lemon. So, 'lebu' is a common descriptor for all citrus fruits. I do not think this interchangeable usage of the word is unique to India though. It seems to me that the various etymological antecedents of lemon in Persian, Arabic and European languages were used to refer to limes or lemons, or limes *and* lemons, or citrus fruits in general. This sort of makes sense given that all citrus fruits are said to be derived from one fruit—the *Citrus medica* or citron. It also strengthens the case for the lemon originating in India.

Early in its life, the English word lemon started being used as a metaphor to denote undesirable things. In Act 5, Scene 2 of Shakespeare's comedy *Love's Labour's Lost*, written in the 1590s, a 'fantastical Spaniard' called Don Armado declares, 'The armipotent Mars, of lances the almighty, Gave Hector a gift—' Three lords, vying to be clever, interrupt him with quippish endings to the sentence. One says that the gift is 'a lemon'. He means it in a negative sense.

A few centuries later, the word also came to refer to an artefact, especially a car, that is substandard or defective. This usage possibly dates back to the 1909 phrase 'the answer's a lemon'. It is derived from the fact that on a fruit machine—a type of casino gambling slot machine—the lemon is the least valuable outcome. The word was used in one of the most successful American ad campaigns of the 1960s: for the Volkswagen Beetle. A print ad had a picture of the car and a one-word headline: 'Lemon'. The body copy explained that the glove compartment of a Beetle was dented, so it did not make the grade. The desired takeaway was that if such a minor flaw could deem a Beetle a lemon, Volkswagen's standards must be high. This and other ads in the campaign made the Volkswagen Beetle a popular car in the USA, despite it being small, ugly and made in a German factory started by Nazis.

In the 1850s, a person with a sour disposition used to be called a lemon. Subsequently, the word also started being used to mean a not-very-bright person who is easily duped: 'I don't know why it is, rich men's sons are always the worst lemons in creation,' wrote comic author P.G. Wodehouse in 1931. Perhaps this term was applied because it is easy to squeeze things out of such individuals—as easy as juicing a lemon.

Why lemons acquired such negative connotations, I do not know. I add lemon—or lime—juice with a pinch of rock salt to the water I drink because it is both delicious and good for the health.

During the Age of Sail, as many as half the sailors on a long voyage would die of a disease called scurvy. It was not known at the time that it was caused by acute vitamin C deficiency. James Lind, a Scottish doctor in the Royal Navy, discovered in

1753 that sailors who were given lemon juice, which is rich in vitamin C, rapidly recovered from the symptoms. In 1795, the Royal Navy was persuaded to provide lemon juice, and later lime juice, to all its sailors—which led to British sailors being nicknamed 'Limeys'. It was a nickname they could live with. After all, limes were what kept them alive.

So, if life gives you lemons—or limes—be like the protagonist of this poem called 'The Optimist' by Clarence Edwin Flynn that appeared in a 1940 edition of *The Rotarian*:

> Life handed him a lemon,
> As Life sometimes will do.
> His friends looked on in pity,
> Assuming he was through.
>
> They came upon him later,
> Reclining in the shade
> In calm contentment, drinking
> A glass of lemonade.

22

Pagoda

Tea
Fragrant leaves, tender buds
The desire of poets, the love of monks
Ground in carved white jade, sifted through red gauze
Cauldron brewed to the colour of gold, bowl aswirl in floral foam
At night it welcomes the bright moon, at daybreak it dispels dawn's rosy mists
Past and present, drinkers are refreshed and tireless, praisefully aware it quells drunkenness

—'Tea' a pagoda poem by Yuan Zhen (779–831)
of the Tang dynasty

As a child, one of the things I was taught to draw in art class was a Chinese pagoda. Note that the structure was described as Chinese. It looked Chinese too—or whatever I assumed at that tender age to be Chinese.

Years later, imagine my surprise when my research into its origin led me to the theory that it was derived from Persian—from *but* (idol) + *kada* (dwelling), a corruption of the word *butkada*. I could not square my notions of Persian antiquity with Chinese traditional architecture.

My surprise was possibly greater when I came across the following definition in the *Oxford English Dictionary*: 'A gold or silver coin of higher denomination than the rupee, formerly current in southern India.' The thought that a pagoda could be an old Indian currency did not intuitively connect with me.

According to this theory, 'pagoda' comes from the Tamil word *pakavati*, derived from Bhagavati in Sanskrit, the name of a Hindu goddess. The image of the goddess was stamped on the coin, hence the name. These coins were possibly used to make offerings to gods in temples—which gave rise to the Portuguese word *pagode*, meaning 'an offering to gods'. As we shall see, this word of the Portuguese—who colonized India—crops up in more than one context.

I came full circle when I became acquainted with a theory of the Chinese etymology of pagoda. It was a relief to find that this was in the architectural sense of the word. Liang Sicheng (1901–72), a scholar of ancient Chinese architecture, pointed out that a pagoda is actually Chinese for 'eight-cornered tower': eight = *pa*, cornered = *ko*, tower = *t'a*. According to him, the eight-cornered tower of the Tomb Pagoda of Ching-tsang, built in 746 CE, was the first true 'pa-go-da'. This was a theory that I instinctively wanted to believe.

The theory gains credibility from the fact that the Portuguese word 'pagode', the precursor of the English 'pagoda', made its debut in 1516—which is around the time pioneer Portuguese seafarers reached China. The spelling 'pagoda' first appeared in Spanish and became known throughout Europe from the translation of Juan Gonzalez de Mendoza's *The History of the Great and Mighty Kingdom of China and the Situation Thereof*, published in 1585. This book was based on the accounts of Portuguese and Spanish missionaries in China.

The octagonal structure of the pagoda is linked to the fact that eight is considered a lucky number in Chinese culture. Originally, pagodas were built as Buddhist temples, after the religion was introduced into the country in the first century. Gradually, however, the pagoda lost its specific religious connotations and by the time of Western contact with China, it had become a cliché of Chinese architecture in general—the reason why I was taught to draw Chinese pagodas in my school in England.

Buddhism spread from India to China, Korea, Japan and Southeast Asia by the first century. In the Southeast Asian countries, it was not just the impact of Buddhism, but a wider and deeper influence of Indian culture that was felt. The stupa took on different forms in these various countries, but it was in China, Korea and Japan that the quintessential pagoda structure emerged.

It must be admitted that the pagoda structure is strikingly absent in India. This makes it hard for some to accept the Indian origin theory. However, the proponents of its Indian etymology will point out that the pagoda is based on the Buddhist stupa, and this type of structure at least, if not the word, has roots in India—like the religion itself.

Perhaps the multiple theories about the word pagoda point to multiple origins. These could have been similar-sounding words with different meanings in different languages that, at some point in history, started influencing each other and getting their narratives intertwined.

The early-ninth-century Chinese 'pagoda poem' whose translation has been provided above actually forms the outline of a pagoda. Let us drink a cup of fragrant Chinese tea as we admire the artistry of the poem and the poetry of the iconic structure that inspired it a millennium ago.

23
Adonis

Is any gentleman in your family and friends' network called an Adonis or a Greek god? Have you ever wondered how the word came to be associated with insanely good-looking men—the Hrithik Roshans of the world?

An Adonis is a handsome young man blessed with almost flawless good looks. The eponym of this word is the Greek god Adonis. The word came into English in the 1620s from Greek, probably via French.

In Greek mythology, Adonis was the great love of the goddess Aphrodite. She even played a key role in his birth, according to one story: she encouraged Myrrha to trick her own father, the Syrian king Theias, to have an incestuous relationship with her. Apparently, this was payback for Theias boasting that his daughter was more beautiful than Aphrodite. When he discovered the deception, Theias went after Myrrha with a knife. Aphrodite turned her into a myrrh tree. Adonis was born from Myrrha-turned-myrrh-tree after Theias shot an arrow into it.

Entranced by the beauty of the infant Adonis, Aphrodite handed him over to Persephone, the queen of the underworld, for safekeeping. As Adonis grew into a beautiful youth, Persephone fell in love with him and refused to return him to Aphrodite. Zeus, the king of the gods, was asked to mediate. He decreed that Adonis should spend four months of the year with Persephone and four months with Aphrodite. He could do as he chose in the remaining four months. Aphrodite seduced Adonis and ensured that he spent those four months also with her.

Adonis died in the prime of his youth when he was gored by a wild boar during a hunt. According to one legend, Persephone engineered this death because she could not bear to let Aphrodite have him. Aphrodite begged Zeus to bring him back to life. Zeus came to a compromise: Adonis would spend half the year with Aphrodite and half in the underworld.

Adonis comes across as a sort of universal boy toy in these stories. Venus, the goddess of love, the counterpart of Aphrodite in Roman mythology, also fell in love with him. In Shakespeare's poem 'Venus and Adonis', Venus describes the attraction she feels towards Adonis thus:

> Had I no eyes but ears, my ears would love
> That inward beauty and invisible;
> Or were I deaf, thy outward parts would move
> Each part in me that were but sensible:
> Though neither eyes nor ears, to hear nor see,
> Yet should I be in love by touching thee

But alas, her love was unrequited, as Adonis was more interested in hunting:

> 'I know not love,' quoth he, 'nor will not know it,
> Unless it be a boar, and then I chase it.

Poor Venus. She was accidentally pricked by her son Cupid's arrow—which had the effect of making you fall in love with the next person you saw. And thus, ironically, the goddess of love fell so one-sidedly in love! The inspiration for this Shakespeare poem was the famous Latin poet Ovid's magnum opus *Metamorphoses*, in which one of the stories was that of Adonis and Venus.

Coming back to Aphrodite, as she wept over the dying Adonis post his hunting accident, she caused anemone flowers to bloom wherever his blood fell—such was the intensity of her tragic love. The heartbroken goddess also declared a festival to be observed on the anniversary of his death.

This is where we move from myth to reality: Adonia was the name given to the festival, which was actually observed by Greek women every year at midsummer from as early as the mid-fifth century BCE. They would plant a 'garden of Adonis'—different fast-growing plants like lettuce and fennel—in a small basket or pot and take it up to their roofs. They would wait for the seeds to rapidly sprout and immediately wither—symbolizing the premature death of Adonis. The women would tear their tunics and beat their breasts, loudly lamenting the death of Aphrodite's consort. They would then immerse a statuette of Adonis, along with the withered plants, in the sea.

The cult of Adonis evolved from the worship of various Near Eastern gods like the Babylonian Tanmuz and Sumerian Dumuzi. They too were consorts of goddesses and suffered from untimely violent deaths. The ritual lamentation of their deaths was similar to the festival of Adonia. 'Adonis' comes from the Phoenician word *adon*, meaning 'lord'. It is also related to Adonai, the Hebrew word for the god of the Bible—a word that is still in use today. The Eastern origin of the Adonis story is consistent with details like the myrrh tree—which does not grow in Greece but in the dry desert lands of Phoenicia.

'The word in poetry must transcend its essence, it must swell and include more,' says celebrated Syrian poet Ali Ahmad Said Esber. For him, words become wombs with a new fertility. He urges us to look beyond surface meanings of words to find universal truths in them. His ideas apply equally to the words of mythology: while we think of beauty, unrequited love and tragedy as the main points of the myth of Adonis, on another level it is about vegetation and the seasons. His death and coming back to life are symbolic of winter and spring and the annual renewal of plant life—phenomena that held deep significance for the agricultural societies of yore.

Incidentally, the pen name of Ali Ahmad Said Esber is Adonis.

24

Chess

'One town's very like another
When your head's down over your pieces, brother'

—'One Night in Bangkok', song from the album *Chess*

Fancy a game of *chaturanga*? You know, the one played by two on a board with 64 alternating black-and-white squares? You probably know the game as chess.

Chess, in its original avatar of chaturanga, was born in India and flourished at least as early as the sixth century. 'Chaturanga' is Sanskrit for 'four limbs'. The term was used in epic poetry to describe the army, which had four arms: elephants, horses, chariots and foot soldiers. It also became the name of a battle-simulation game inspired in part by the Mahabharata. This ultimately evolved into the modern game of chess.

It is said that the mathematical sophistication of ancient India, as evinced by the invention of zero, led to the creation of board games like chess. Chaturanga was devised for the 8 x 8 all-white board called *ashtapada* in Sanskrit—literally meaning 'eight-footed'. Makruk, the Thai version of chess, and the Cambodian ouk-chaktrang, still played on uncheckered boards, are the closest surviving relatives of the original form of chaturanga.

The Arab historian Abu al-Hasan Ali al-Masudi writes that chess was introduced into Persia from India. It came into the country along with the book *Kelileh va Demneh*, possibly a translation of the *Panchatantra*, a collection of Sanskrit animal fables, during the reign of Emperor Nushirwan. Masudi claims that Indians used chess in mathematics, gambling and astronomy, and as a tool for military strategy.

The original pieces over which two players broke their heads were made of ivory and ebony. They consisted of the *raja* (king), *mantri* (adviser), *gaja* (elephant), *asva* (horse), *ratha* (chariot)— or *roka* (boat)—and *padati* (foot soldier). In the present-day English version of the game, the adviser has become the queen, the elephant is the bishop, the horse is the knight, the boat—the Sanskrit 'roka'—is the rook, and the padati or foot soldier, the pawn. What was unique to the game of chaturanga—and which is retained in chess—is that the different pieces have different powers and the outcome of the game depends on one piece, the king. This separates chess from other board games like checkers, in which all the pieces of a colour look and act the same.

Around 600 CE, Persian royalty learnt the game from Indians. They pronounced it as 'chatrang', played it for a couple of centuries, and taught it to the Arabs. The latter did not have the 'ch' or 'ng' sounds in their language, so they started pronouncing it as 'shatranj'. When they invaded Spain in 711 CE, they took the game with them; that is how Europe got chess—the game, not the word.

The Moroccan Arabs who took *shatranj* to Spain by the tenth century pronounced it as 'shatarej', which ultimately became the Spanish word for chess, *ajedrez*. However, if you thought that the English word chess is derived from 'ajedrez', you would be wrong. 'Chess' is derived from the Persian word for king, 'shah', which is what the Persians renamed the raja of chaturanga. The Arabs borrowed the word shah from the Persians. And that gave rise to the different words for chess in various European languages, apart from Spanish.

In a game of chess, when the king or shah of your opponent is 'in check'—meaning, in danger of being captured—you warn your opponent by saying 'check'. 'Check' comes from the Old French word *eschec*, meaning 'a check'. Its plural form, *eschés*, gave rise to the modern French word for chess, *échecs*. It also spawned the Middle English 'ches' or 'chesse'—which morphed into the modern English word 'chess'.

Odd as it sounds, the old French word 'eschec' came from 'shah', via *scaccus* in Vulgar Latin. It is easier to accept this etymology if you consider the related term 'checkmate': when the king is in check, with no way to get out of this tight spot, the player is said to be checkmated. In algebraic notation, this move is described by the # sign—a visualization of the king being trapped from all sides. A checkmate signals the end of the game. At this point, you might hear the winner triumphantly announce, 'Checkmate!' The Persians or Arabs would have said, '*Shah-mat!*' This meant 'the king is helpless' or 'the king is dead'. 'Shah-mat' became 'check-mate'. This term is so fundamental to chess that, when the game spread from the Middle East to Russia, it actually came to be known as *shakhmaty*, literally 'checkmates'.

In the original chaturanga, the game ended when the king was captured. The Persian royalty who took up the game decided it wise to warn the player whose king was in danger of being captured by calling out, 'Shah!' While playing in English we call out 'check' for the same reason.

Shahnameh, the eleventh-century Persian epic poem by Ferdowsi, has an account of a visiting Indian king who re-enacted ancient battles using chess. The Persians thought it was a great idea. Thanks to them, till today the entire world plays the war-strategy game based on the Indian epic Mahabharata.

25

Ammonia

I dimly remember a test question from class eight: name a compound of nitrogen and hydrogen that is a colourless gas with a sharp smell...

Chemistry was not my strongest subject, but I had long been intrigued by the concept of smelling salts, having read about them in the guffaw-inducing pages of P.G. Wodehouse's Jeeves and Wooster books.

The ladies of Wodehousian England seemed to always have smelling salts handy in case the goings-on around them made them feel faint—which they frequently did. These fictional recurrences piqued my curiosity enough for me to find out more about the salts that the ladies inhaled to regain their consciousness.

It turns out that smelling salts are essentially ammonia—which, of course, explains their consciousness-reviving aroma. And so, thanks to Wodehouse, I was conscious of the properties of good old NH_3, and was thus able to get the answer to at least one chemistry test question right.

We get the word 'ammonia' from 'sal ammoniac', which is the old name for ammonium chloride. *Sal ammoniacus*, the Latin form of sal ammoniac, literally means 'salt of Ammon'. It has this name because it was first discovered near the temple of Amun, the Egyptian god of life and reproduction. Amun was rendered as Ammon by the Romans, and equated with their god Jupiter after they conquered North Africa. According to one story, worshippers would 'park' their camels when they stopped to pray at this shrine. Enterprising locals would sell the dung-infused sand for its sal ammoniac content. Apparently, ammonia is still made from camel dung in modern Egypt.

The ancient Greek historian Herodotus (c. 484–425 BCE) wrote about salt deposits in an area of ancient Egypt whose inhabitants he called Ammonians. Salt lakes still exist in this desert area of northwestern Egypt, known as the Siwa oasis. The Greek geographer Strabo also mentioned the salt from this region. Whether this salt was sal ammoniac has not been established. Roman philosopher and naturalist Pliny the Elder (23–79 CE) mentions *hammoniacus sal* in his writings. It is not clear, though, if this old term meant the same as sal ammoniac.

In the thirteenth century, Albert Magnus (1200–80), the great German theologian, mentioned sal ammoniac in the context of alchemy, in a way that is clearly associated with ammonia. According to the *Oxford English Dictionary*, the earliest mention of it in Middle English was around 1325, in *Chronicle of England*.

In the fifteenth century, alchemist Basil Valentine of Germany—recognized as the father of modern chemistry—produced ammonia by reacting alkalis with sal ammoniac. Later, for a time, ammonia became known as 'spirit of hartshorn' as people took to preparing it by distilling the nitrogen-laden hoofs and horns of deer and other animals. It was also known as 'volatile alkali' or 'animal alkali'—to distinguish it from vegetable or mineral alkali.

In 1774, ammonia gas was isolated by Joseph Priestley, the famous English chemist, theologian and grammarian. He called it 'alkaline air'. Around 1785, French chemist Claude Louis Berthollet determined its composition. The term ammonia itself was coined, as a derivation from sal ammoniac, by Swedish chemist Torbern Bergman in 1782.

The reason so many have fussed about ammonia since ancient times is that it was, and continues to be, a useful chemical—and not just as smelling salts, mind you. Mentioned by the Persian-Arab chemist Jabir ibn Hayyan, sal ammoniac was important even to eighth-century Muslim alchemists. Produced in antiquity by fermenting urine with bacteria, it was used in preparing hides for tanning, cleaning and dyeing cloth and removing rust from iron.

It is not an exaggeration to say that ammonia altered the course of history. German chemists Fritz Haber and Karl Bosch devised a process to mass produce ammonia by directly combining nitrogen and hydrogen—considered one of the biggest technological advancements of the twentieth century. It paved the way for the mass production of fertilizer, in which ammonia is a key ingredient, thereby transforming agriculture and increasing the world's food supply. During World War I, it strengthened Germany's position by ensuring that the country had a plentiful supply of both fertilizer and explosive—the latter also being produced from ammonia.

Today, ammonia is used to manufacture many useful things, including pharmaceutical and cleaning products—making our world a healthier, more hygienic one. So, while we may wrinkle our noses at its smell, we certainly cannot disdain its importance in our lives.

26

Sardonic

If you are a fan of Batman, you would be familiar with Joker Venom. It is the villainous Joker's signature murder weapon, a toxin that makes his victims uncontrollably laugh their way to their painful deaths.

This is fiction, right? Or...is it?

Around the turn of the century, a Sardinian shepherd was found dead, with a ghastly grin on his face. Investigations showed that he had committed suicide by eating a poisonous plant called hemlock water dropwort.

If we went back almost three millennia, we might have found more such grinning corpses in Sardinia, the scenic Italian island. There existed a custom of killing off criminals or elderly people who could no longer look after themselves. The chosen method was the administration of a poisonous herb that apparently made the victims fall into fits of laughter while dying, leaving behind a corpse with a frozen smile. Of course, the toxin was not administered in the form of a gas like the Joker's, but its effects were similar. Also, the islanders did not take any chances. They intoxicated the victims with the herb and then either beat them to death or threw them from a high rock. The word 'sardonic', which has come to mean 'unkind, mocking humour', originates from this ancient Sardinian practice.

The mind boggles at the mindset behind this custom, so one will, instead, focus on other details.

The victims' death smile was described as a 'sardonic grin'

by Homer in the eighth century BCE. *Sardanios*, the old Greek root of the word sardonic, appeared in his epic the Odyssey. It was then modified by association with the Greek word for Sardinian, *Sardonios*, which had such lovely connotations as 'being sneered at', 'the tearing of flesh' and 'scornful laughter'. From there we get the Latin *sardonius*, the French *sardonique* and, finally, the English sardonic. The sardonic grin is also referred to in the *Suda*, a tenth-century Greek encyclopaedia of the Mediterranean region.

According to the *Oxford English Dictionary*, the earliest recorded use of the adjective sardonic in English dates to 1638. This citation is from the writings of Thomas Herbert, an English traveller and writer. In his book *Some Yeares Travels into Divers Parts of Asia and Afrique*, Herbert writes, 'He... gives a Sardonick smile to think how blest hee was in this attonement.' This early English usage of the term denotes a grim, mocking smile, one which indicates perhaps that the 'blessing' of this atonement is not so blessed after all.

Risus sardonicus, which is Latin for 'scornful laughter', is also applied to the fake smile that results from the muscular spasms of the face in those afflicted with tetanus or strychnine poisoning. The eyebrows rise, the eyes bulge and the mouth is stretched back in an exaggerated Joker-like grin.

Incidentally, the Joker's look may be inspired by the Glasgow smile—an exaggerated smiling appearance created by making a cut from the corners of one's mouth up to the ears. This was a signature of Scottish criminals in the 1920s but was later adopted by English street gangs such as the Chelsea Headhunters. Thus it was renamed the Chelsea Smile. The British rock group Bring Me the Horizon had a song called 'Chelsea Smile' in its 2008 album *Suicide Season*—which, of course, has nothing to do with the Sardinian suicide. The song has such charming lyrics as

'I may look happy, but honestly dear / The only way I'll really smile is if you cut me ear to ear'.

The shepherd's suicide gave us a clue to the identity of the 'sardonic herb'. For centuries, it was a mystery. But the death by consuming hemlock water dropwort led to fresh research into its toxic effects. The researchers concluded that this must be the plant that the ancients referred to as the sardonic herb. In the entire Mediterranean region, it is only in Sardinia that the plant grows. And it flourishes in the moist climate of the areas in which the ritual killings used to take place.

Who knew that when paired with the word sardonic, something as benign as a smile could be linked with poisonous herbs, fictional villains and ritual killings?

27

Mesmerize

Franz Anton Mesmer, a German-born physician in eighteenth-century Vienna, achieved prestige, fame, fortune—and then lost it all, ending his days in infamy, poverty and exile. Today he is remembered mainly because of the verb derived from his name—'mesmerize'—which means 'to hypnotize'.

So how did his life take this trajectory? Well, to start with, Mesmer came up with a theory he called 'animal gravitation'. He posited that there are tides in our bodies—which are affected by solar and lunar gravitation, with implications for our health. Later, his focus shifted from gravitation to magnetism, and he renamed his theory 'animal magnetism'. He spoke of an invisible fluid that flows through the body, positing that when this flow is impeded, people fall ill. He had developed a technique with which, he claimed, he could normalize the flow.

His therapeutic approach was called Mesmerism. Initially he treated patients one on one. He would induce a 'crisis' in them: they would experience convulsions. After the convulsions passed, they would be cured. In 1774 he treated a 28-year-old patient, Franziska Österlin, who suffered from 'hysterical' ailments—episodic pain, convulsions, etc. Mesmer had her swallow a solution containing iron and then applied magnets to her body, aiming to realign an invisible fluid in her nerves. The result was dramatic: Österlin felt mysterious 'streams' of energy coursing through her and experienced relief from her symptoms for a time. She became the first person ever to be 'mesmerized' and cured—at least temporarily—of her medical troubles.

As his fame spread, hundreds, if not thousands, of patients flocked to him, and he had to resort to group sessions to handle the load.

In 1768, Mesmer married a wealthy widow, set himself up as a doctor in Vienna, and also became a patron of the arts. He was a benefactor to Wolfgang Amadeus Mozart. The prolific Austrian composer reciprocated by immortalizing Mesmer through a reference to him in his opera *Così fan tutte*.

Things started to unravel when Mesmer attempted to cure Maria Theresia von Paradis, a famous blind musician. His treatment met with partial success, but this created a new problem. The 18-year-old girl's family was concerned that she would lose the financial support she received from Queen Empress Maria Theresa on account of her blindness. Hence, they declared that despite Mesmer's treatment, Maria remained completely blind, and her condition had also deteriorated under the physician's care.

This came as a blow to Mesmer. Since he did not enjoy the support of the medical establishment, he had taken on this high-profile case to prove his expertise. However, things backfired and tarnished his reputation further among the medical fraternity. With the ensuing controversy, he was deemed a fraud and compelled to leave Vienna. This was in 1778. He moved to Paris where he once again developed a thriving practice.

One lady-in-waiting at Queen Marie Antoinette's court, who had been paralysed, credited Mesmer with her recovery and appealed to the queen to officially endorse his methods. Such reports won Mesmer influential patrons, including Princess de Lamballe, the Prince de Condé and the young Marquis de

Lafayette. All of them vouched for the apparently miraculous cures. By 1780, Mesmer was the toast of Paris, treating rich and poor alike. He even opened a free clinic for the poor and boasted that his magnetism could cure virtually any disease.

Then, in 1784, King Louis XVI of France set up a commission to investigate the validity of the invisible fluid that Mesmer claimed to have discovered and which was at the heart of his theory of animal magnetism. The commissioners were prominent personages such as the chemist Antoine Lavoisier, the doctor Joseph-Ignace Guillotin (after whom the guillotine is named) and the American ambassador Benjamin Franklin. They concluded that Mesmer's invisible fluid did not exist. Mesmer was devastated by this pronouncement.

The story of Mesmer has an Indian connection too. Abbé Faria, a Goan Catholic monk, was one of the pioneers of the scientific study of hypnosis. A contemporary of Mesmer's, Faria too discounted the theory of animal magnetism, declaring that all the effects of his treatment came from within the imagination of the patient; in other words, the results of autosuggestion.

While Mesmer may have been deemed a quack by the medical, academic and political authorities of his day with his theory disproved, the fact is that he did manage to help many patients with his technique. The conventional medicine of his day had very little to offer and it is quite possible that the establishment attacked him out of envy, precisely because he was successful.

Given that science today has accepted the interconnectedness of mind and body, the concept of curing a patient by mesmerizing them should be considered something of value, in my opinion.

In fact, with hindsight, historians and medical experts now view Mesmer's reported cures as early examples of psychological healing. Mesmer's charismatic presence and elaborate rituals effectively mobilized the placebo effect and his patients cured themselves through the power of suggestion—making Mesmer an unwitting pioneer of hypnotherapy.

28

Khaki

The British Army's scarlet tunic may have looked smart, but it was not suited to India's torrid climate. The optional white uniform was also not ideal in India's heat and dust. And both colours were easy to spot by the enemy.

Which is why, in 1846, when Lieutenant Harry Lumsden was given the job of forming the Corps of Guides, a new regiment of infantry and cavalry soldiers, he decided to come up with a more practical uniform.

Lumsden was based in the northwestern part of British India. To come up with a suitable uniform, he experimented with loose-fitting cotton garments based on the local men's attire. He had them dyed a muddy tan colour that hid the dirt and helped the soldiers be less conspicuous on the dusty battlefields.

And thus, khaki was born.

The word 'khaki' comes from the Persian and Urdu word *khak*, meaning 'dust' or 'soil'. Khaki literally means 'dust' or 'earth-coloured'. And so, cloth dyed in this colour came to be known as khaki to the Indian soldiers. And the British picked up the term from them.

Initially, the khaki uniforms were scoffed at. British soldiers from other regiments nicknamed the Corps of Guides 'mudlarks' because of the muddy colour of their uniforms. But it did not take long for British officers to realize the practicality of this colour, and it was adopted by other regiments as well—especially during the Sepoy Mutiny of 1857.

The khaki colour was achieved at first by dunking the fabric in mud. Lumsden and his soldiers may also have experimented with a local dye made from the Mazari palm as well as with soaking the fabric in tea, coffee, curry powder or tobacco juice to achieve the khaki colour.

But with the rise of the textile industry, a synthetic khaki dye was developed. It was registered in England in 1884. But soon the British found it cheaper to import khaki dye from Germany, and by the time World War I happened, the British found themselves in the embarrassing situation of importing most of the khaki dye for their soldiers' uniforms from the enemy country.

Khaki spread around the world with the British Army. In fact, during the Anglo-Boer war in South Africa from 1899 to 1902, British troops were referred to as 'khakis' because of the colour of their uniform. The term 'khaki election' also came into being at that time. A khaki election is an election that is influenced by wartime or post-war sentiment. The British general election in the year 1900 was one such. It was heavily influenced by the Anglo-Boer war.

Khaki spread from the British Army to the American military, and eventually spread to civilian populations in both countries. Khaki clothing could be found in shops in England in the early 1900s. The heroic connotations of the colour appealed to Victorian gentlemen. And in America, after World War I, especially in the era of the Great Depression, khaki became the standard civilian work clothing.

When khaki was adopted by the British Army as their continental service dress, they introduced a darker shade with a green hue. This colour too is accepted as khaki.

While khaki cloth was all cotton at first, it was later also made with wool or a combination of cotton and wool, and eventually with blends of synthetic fibres. It was made in various weaves such as serge.

Khaki became synonymous with the police force in India and continues to be so. The word has entered popular culture as well, finding its way into the titles of Bollywood movies and web series.

Khaki gained in popularity around the world, particularly in the US, as it became associated not just with soldiers but also with explorers, adventurers and other famous men of the twentieth century. Here are some of the famous Americans who wore 'khakis', as khaki trousers started being called: Aviator Charles Lindbergh, who made the first non-stop flight from New York to Paris, the first-ever solo transatlantic flight, wore them. World-famous American authors Ernest Hemingway and Jack Kerouac did as well. President John F. Kennedy was fond of his khakis. Actors John Wayne and James Dean wore the fabled pants. The fondness for khakis was not restricted just to the men of the silver screen; Katharine Hepburn too was a big fan of them. These famous wearers gave khakis an irresistible aura and by the 1950s, they became standard clothing for young Americans. And, in the 1980s, the Dockers brand launched its iconic khaki pants as a more comfortable option for office wear—leading to the phenomenon of Casual Fridays, a more relaxed approach to dressing for work.

Khaki had undergone quite an image change since India introduced it to the world. What came to be considered fashionable started out as a fabric that was thought to be practical but ugly, even by its supporters. A correspondent for *The Times of India* wrote in 1861, 'Although khakee is hideous in its appearance I have not the slightest doubt it has contributed to save the lives of many brave men who would otherwise have fallen victim to the severity of the climate.' In 1883, the same paper quoted a regimental newspaper to say that having to wear khaki, 'an expensive, ill-wearing material, which makes [the wearer] ashamed of himself', is the second biggest reason—the first being low pay—that British soldiers did not like serving in India.

And to think that today khaki trousers are to be found in the closet of almost every fashionable man—and many fashionable women—around the world!

29

Berserk

I came across a video game the other day called *Berserk Mode*. It invited you to 'Become the Berserker, an unstoppable paragon of violence'. It led me to wonder what 'berserk' really means.

We often talk about going berserk. For example, 'The cricket fans went berserk when their team lost.' This means that the fans went out of control with anger. They became unruly. Perhaps even violent.

Now let's look at the opposite scenario: 'The cricket fans went berserk when their team won.' In this case, the fans were out of control with excitement. They probably went a bit crazy in a joyful way.

Here are some more examples:

'The dog went berserk after it was stung by a wasp.'
'Dev will go berserk when he discovers that his son dropped his new phone and cracked its screen.'
'The little girl goes berserk every time she enters the ice-cream shop.'
'What if robots go berserk and start attacking humans?'

From these examples, we can gather that berserk means 'out of control with anger or excitement'. To go berserk is to go crazy or behave in a frenzied manner.

Berserk is an unusual sounding word. This is not surprising given its unusual origin.

Berserk comes from 'berserker'—the word I came across

in the video game description. Berserker originated in the Old Norse language from which Norwegian and other Scandinavian languages originated. In Old Norse literature, berserkers were those who fought in a trance-like fury. This mental state was probably enhanced with drugs and alcohol.

Berserk and berserker are derived from the Old Norse word *bersekr*, meaning 'raging warrior of superhuman strength'—this is not too different from the video game description of the berserker as an 'unstoppable paragon of violence'. The word was introduced into English by Sir Walter Scott through his book *The Pirate* in 1822, spelt as 'berserkar'. Even today, one of the meanings of berserk in English is 'an invulnerable ancient Scandinavian warrior who is frenzied in battle'.

Sir Walter Scott was a Scottish writer. He was the most widely-read novelist of the early nineteenth century. He is the inventor of the historical novel, and his works are considered classics of European and Scottish literature. These include novels like *Ivanhoe*, *Rob Roy* and *Waverley* as well as poems like 'The Lady of the Lake'. Scott's *The Pirate* is set in the Shetland Islands, which are the northernmost point of the United Kingdom. This archipelago is just 230 km west of Bergen, Norway. Historically, these islands were under Norwegian rule. Scott believed that 'berserk' was derived from the Old Norse *berr*, meaning 'bare' or 'naked', plus *serk*, meaning 'shirt'. So, he took the word to mean 'bare-shirt'—a warrior who went into battle without his armour.

However, the more accepted view is that berserk means 'bear-shirt'—someone who wears a bearskin coat and not the coat of mail that other Norse warriors wore in battle. Imagine a Scandinavian warrior in a bearskin coat going berserk—the enemy must have retreated in fright! These berserkers were said to have been the elite warriors of Harald Fairhair, the first king of Norway and, according to legend, of Odin, the supreme Norse deity. The frenzy and ferocity of the berserkers are described in Norse sagas. They gnawed at their shields, foamed at the mouth and roared like wild beasts to terrify their opponents. According to the thirteenth-century Icelandic historian Snorri Sturluson, 'They killed people, and neither fire nor iron did them any harm.' This, he said, 'is called berserk rage.'

So that was what going berserk was originally all about. The video game I mentioned earlier is obviously inspired by this ancient form of berserk rage. The introduction to the game asks you, the player, to 'navigate the sublime depths of your battle-trance in a storm of blood and gibs. Prepare to enter Berserk Mode.' 'Gibs', I learnt, is short for 'giblets'. The word giblets refers to organs like the liver, heart, neck, kidneys and gizzard of a bird which are often removed before cooking. But in gaming slang, gibs refers to blowing up your enemy and scattering their body parts! Gruesome!

But a video game is still a safe way to satisfy one's urge to go berserk. On the other hand, something like road rage—which is angry or aggressive behaviour while driving—is dangerous as it can escalate with motorists going berserk, leading to terrible accidents in the real world.

Citing my own case, I'm known to go berserk when I spot grammatical errors.

30
Assassin

An assassination is the murder of a public figure. It usually refers to the killing of a head of state or other prominent person for political motives. The reasons behind the killing could be to undermine a government, grab power, take revenge, get attention for a cause, or start a revolution.

The person who carries out an assassination is called an assassin. You may have played the action-adventure video game *Assassin's Creed*. Or watched the film based on it. But have you ever wondered where the word 'assassin' comes from?

The word assassin is possibly derived from the Arabic word *hashshashin*, which was used to refer to a religious sect of Ismaili Shi'a Muslims of the Nizari lineage that originated in Persia in the eleventh century CE. Its original leader was Hassan al-Sabbah, a missionary from Egypt. He ran his secret society of Hashshashins or Assassins from his stronghold in Alamut in northern Persia. At its peak the community extended to Egypt, Syria, Yemen, southern Iraq, southwest Iran and Afghanistan.

The Assassins would defeat their enemies not with a large army but by deploying individuals who would infiltrate enemy strongholds and use subterfuge to kill key military and political leaders. They were masters of disguise and usually used knives to carry out the killings. The Assassins employed their techniques against their rivals in the Muslim world as well as European Crusaders. The latter were Christians who fought in the Middle Ages to win the Holy Lands from Muslims.

The word 'hashshashin' means 'consumer of hashish'. Hashish is a drug derived from the cannabis plant. Enemies of the Assassins may have attributed their ability to strike at their opponents so effectively—as well as their willingness to die for the cause—to the use of hashish. Or it may simply have been a derogatory term applied to them without any basis in actual drug use. In other words, it may have been like calling someone a pothead in order to demean them. Later, the word hashshashin lost its original connection to drugs and started being used in the sense of 'outlaw'. And in Egypt in the 1930s, it was used to mean 'noisy' or 'riotous'.

The Venetian merchant and traveller Marco Polo wrote about the Assassins. He mentioned that the young boys who were being trained as assassins were given intoxicants and taken to a secret paradisical garden by the leaders of the sect. The boys were given this experience of paradise as a taste of things to come in the afterlife if they successfully carried out their missions.

There is another school of thought that the derivation of assassin has nothing to do with hashish but simply means a follower of Hassan. As noted earlier, the first leader of the Assassins was Hassan al-Sabbah. According to texts from Alamut, Hassan called his disciples 'Assassiyun', meaning people faithful to the 'Assass'—the 'foundation' of the faith. 'Assassin' may actually have come from 'Assassiyun'.

The Assassins finally met their match when they tried to assassinate the Mongol leader Möngke Khan, grandson of Gengis Khan. The Mongols went after them and defeated them in 1256 in Alamut. Though the Assassins managed to retake Alamut, they lost it again. With most of their strongholds gone, they operated independently for another century as contract killers. But they disappeared eventually.

The Crusaders brought home to Europe stories about the militant Ismaili sect within the Nizaris, and their nickname Hashshashin entered European languages. The word became *assassini* in Italian and entered English as 'assassin' in the 1530s. By that time, the original meaning of the word was long forgotten. The generalization of the sect's nickname to mean an assassin in the modern sense had already happened in Italian in the early fourteenth century.

The verb 'assassinate' was first recorded in English in 1600 in a pamphlet by Matthew Sutcliffe titled *A Briefe Replie to a Certaine Odious and Slanderous Libel, Lately Published by a Seditious Jesuite*. The noun 'assassination' appeared sometime later in Act 1, Scene 7 of Shakespeare's *Macbeth*, which was first printed in 1603:

> If it were done when 'tis done, then 'twere well
> It were done quickly: if the assassination
> Could trammel up the consequence, and catch
> With his surcease success; that but this blow
> Might be the be-all and the end-all here,
> But here, upon this bank and shoal of time,
> We'd jump the life to come.

Assassinations have been used as a tool of power politics throughout recorded history. The first known victim of an assassination is said to be the Egyptian pharaoh Teti. This assassination would have taken place c. 2333 BCE.

Chanakya wrote about assassinations in *Arthashastra*, his famous political treatise. His student Chandragupta Maurya, who founded the Maurya dynasty in India, used assassinations to eliminate some of his enemies. In his book *The Art of War*, the Chinese general Sun Tzu too wrote about assassinations as an effective political tool. Two millennia later, Italian diplomat

Machiavelli wrote in his book *The Prince* that it was advisable to assassinate enemies whenever possible so that they couldn't trouble you anymore.

The assassination of Archduke Franz Ferdinand in Austria in 1914 precipitated World War I. The assassin was a Serbian nationalist called Gavrilo Princip. Closer to home, Mahatma Gandhi was assassinated in 1948. His assassin was Nathuram Godse. Prime ministers Indira Gandhi and Rajiv Gandhi were also assassinated in 1984 and 1991, respectively.

You don't always have to be a political leader for your murder to be considered an assassination. In 2006, investigative reporter Anna Politkovskaya—a critic of Vladimir Putin—was shot and killed in Moscow. She is one of the many journalists who have been assassinated during the Putin regime. Maurizio Gucci, the one-time head of the Gucci fashion house, was assassinated in 1995. Investigations revealed that the murder was carried out at his former wife's behest.

So, from a word meaning 'hashish-eater', which was applied as a term of abuse for a sect in medieval Persia and Syria, we get the English word assassin, meaning 'a murderer of public figures'.

Stories of Phrases

31

Teddy bear

'If you go down in the woods today
You're sure of a big surprise
If you go down in the woods today
You better go in disguise!
For every bear that ever there was
Will gather there for certain
Because today's the day the
Teddy bears have their picnic'

—'The Teddy Bears' Picnic' (1932), Jimmy Kennedy

He is the youngest man ever to become the president of the United States of America. His face is carved on Mount Rushmore. As historical and contemporary records show, he is one of the most popular American presidents, beloved to people the world over.

Yet, arguably, rather than with his robust foreign policy, the great man's name is more commonly associated with stuffed, cuddly toy bears.

I refer to Theodore Roosevelt, the twenty-sixth US president, who assumed office at the age of 42 in 1901 and served till 1909. Soon after he became president, Roosevelt was invited to a bear hunt in Mississippi by Governor Andrew H. Longino. Most of the other hunters on the trip had killed bears already, so Roosevelt's attendants decided to help the president bag one too. They caught, injured and tied an American black bear to a tree and suggested that Roosevelt shoot it. The former president found this unsportsmanlike and declined.

This story spread like wildfire and, on 16 November 1902, it became the subject of a political cartoon in *The Washington Post*. Drawn by Pulitzer prize-winning cartoonist Clifford Berryman, it depicted a bear lassoed by a handler as the president looked on in disgust. While this original cartoon featured an adult black bear, in later drawings it was replaced with a younger, cuter bear.

Brooklyn candy-shop owner Morris Michtom and his wife Rose also made stuffed toys. They were inspired by the cartoon to create a stuffed toy bear cub. Michtom put it in his shop window with the sign 'Teddy's Bear'—'Teddy' being the traditional American nickname for 'Theodore'. The bear was a hit with the public and there was demand for many more. Taking the president's permission to use his name, Michtom decided to mass produce the toy bears. He soon founded the Ideal Novelty and Toy Co.—which became the largest doll-making company in America.

Apart from fuelling a boom in stuffed toys, Teddy's bears helped change the image of wild animals in the public imagination. They were no longer dangerous and fearsome beasts, but creatures that should be protected and perhaps even cuddled, thus contributing to wildlife conservation consciousness in America.

Teddy's bears, which soon came to be known simply as 'teddy bears', became a part of the cultural fabric. In 1905, American author Seymour Eaton published *The Roosevelt Bears: Their Travels and Adventures* as a serialized story in newspapers. Its protagonists Teddy-B and Teddy-G go on a train trip to see

America. Thanks to their exploits along the way they become famous, get media coverage, and acquire a following. The following year, a comic illustrated poem inspired by Roosevelt's conservationist zeal appeared in *The New York Times*. It too featured two bears named Teddy, and inspired the naming of two real bears presented to the Bronx Zoo that year. In 1907, composer John Walter Bratton wrote an instrumental piece called 'The Teddy Bears' Picnic'. Irish lyricist Jimmy Kennedy set lyrics to it in 1932. The first two stanzas of it are featured above.

Meanwhile, in Germany, Richard Steiff—who knew nothing about the American craze for teddy bears—had designed his own plush toy bear codenamed Steiff Bear 55PB. After it was exhibited at the Leipzig Toy Fair in 1903, an American buyer ordered 3,000 pieces. These were manufactured by the Steiff company, owned by Richard's aunt Margarete Steiff. The following year, the Steiffs sold 12,000 of their bears at the St. Louis World's Fair, giving a German angle to the American story of the teddy bear.

With extended snouts and beady eyes, the early teddy bears looked more like real bears. As time went by, they were given more baby-like features—snub snouts, bigger eyes and wider foreheads—as these were thought to make the bears cuter.

In child psychology, a teddy bear plays the role of a 'transitional object'—something that helps provide psychological comfort to a child as it develops from a phase of complete dependence on its mother to one of relative independence—the reason why many children around the world cuddle a teddy bear when they go to bed. When I was a child, I persuaded my mother to buy me a teddy bear. And I still have that furry little honey-brown bear with adorable amber and black eyes after all these years—perhaps indicating that I never really grew up!

32
White elephant

> 'Lucky you, you're #1
> You get to start all the fun.
> So grab a gift and grab it quick.
> 'Cause you're the one who gets first pick.'
>
> —'White Elephant Poem', Anonymous

Have you ever received useless gifts that you did not know what to do with? If you get married in India, you get multiple 51-piece plastic storage container sets. Public speakers get gigantic vases as 'a token of appreciation' almost every time they deliver a speech. And, if you have friends who go on seaside vacations without you, you may have been gifted not-so-attractive and cheap baubles made of seashells.

What do you do with this stuff you have no use or room for? Some Westerners play a party game called the White Elephant Gift Exchange—allegedly popularized around 1828 by Ezra Cornell, philanthropist and founder of Western Union. In this game, players recycle useless gifts, passing them on to a friend. This is done for the sake of amusement. The fun only lasts for the duration of the party though, because you still go home with a useless gift, albeit different from the one you had earlier.

The prevalent theory of the origin of the term 'white

elephant' is that the king of Siam—the old name for Thailand—used to gift white elephants to courtiers he was displeased with. These were actually rare albino elephants that were not quite white, but of a pinkish hue. You could not put the animal to work as it was considered sacred. Nor could you get rid of it, as that would anger the king even more. With the high cost of the animal's upkeep, the courtiers would be financially ruined. Thus, 'white elephant' came to mean an impractical gift that is hard to maintain or dispose of. (However, this origin theory cannot be right. As we shall see later in this chapter, white elephants were considered far too precious in Southeast Asia to have been gifted to people as a punitive measure.)

An ad in *The Derbyshire Times* on 30 September 1933 came to the aid of recipients of such gifts:

> ELEPHANTS
> of almost any colour, except
> the pink kind, can easily
> be disposed of through
> OUR SMALL
> ADVTS.
> GET RID OF YOUR
> WHITE ELEPHANTS
> by sending a Small
> Advt. to
> "The Derbyshire Times,"
> Station Road, Chesterfield.

The phrase was in common use by the nineteenth century. It was likely popularized by P.T. Barnum, the American showman who funded the Barnum & Bailey Circus. He spent a lot of money to acquire Toung Taloung, the animal he described as the 'sacred white elephant' of Burma. This elephant turned out to have a dirty grey complexion with only a smattering of pink, disappointing its buyer.

One of the early references in English to the idiomatic 'white elephant' is in an essay titled 'Of false Honour, publick and private', published in the *London Journal* on 16 December 1721. This was one of a series of essays written by British writers John Trenchard and Thomas Gordon that were later published in the form of a book called *Cato's Letters*. After describing a bloody war fought by the king of Pegu against the king of Siam—to acquire a white elephant the latter had refused to sell him—the essay has this to say: '...Honour and Victory are generally no more than white Elephants; and for white Elephants the most destructive Wars have been often made.'

From this essay, one can also surmise that a pale pachyderm was hardly seen as a burden, at least in these Asian societies. On the contrary, it was so coveted that wars were fought over it. The high value that people put on it was partly due to the rarity of the white or albino elephant in nature. Not only did it signal the power, prestige and wealth of its owner, but it was also considered holy. In Buddhist lore, it was said that a white elephant appeared before Mahamaya, Lord Buddha's mother, the night he was born.

White elephants were kept by the rulers of Burma, Thailand, Laos and Cambodia. So important was the elephant to them that they incorporated the equivalent of 'Lord of the White Elephant' in their titles. The monarchs of Burma and Thailand keep white elephants to this day.

It is interesting to note that 'white elephant' is an imperfect translation of *chang pheuak*, the Thai name for this creature. 'Chang' means 'elephant'. But 'pheuak' means 'strange-coloured' and not white. Given the actual colour of the albino elephant, 'pink pachyderm' might have been a better way to describe it. Pink or white, I wonder if the reverence for this pale-complexioned animal has something to do with the fairness obsession among people in Asia.

Today, a white elephant does not only mean a useless gift. It refers to any possession whose cost of purchase or maintenance is disproportionate to its utility. It could mean an expensive building project—such as a sports facility made for a one-time international event—or a business venture that appears magnificent but does not live up to expectations.

Here's how you can use the idiomatic expression in a sentence:

> 'What was meant to be a grand resort in suburban Mumbai is now a white elephant crumbling with neglect.'
> 'She inherited a haveli from her uncle, but with all the repairs and taxes, it turned into a white elephant.'
> 'I bought a treadmill during a fitness resolution frenzy, used it for a week, and now it's a white elephant doubling as a glorified coat hanger!'

33
Caught red-handed

> 'I stole only once in my life, at five years old:
> an apple snatched through the neighbour's window.
> A satin-skinned, sugar-apple whose mother was moonlight
> and whose father was the sun.
> I was caught red-handed.'
>
> —'Stolen Apple', Farzaneh Khojandi
> (Translated from Tajik by Narguess Farzad
> and Jo Shapcott)

Thanks to CCTV cameras, it is much easier to catch criminals red-handed nowadays. But in fifteenth-century Scotland, if thieves stole and slaughtered your livestock, you had to catch them with the blood of the dead animal on their hands to establish that they were the perpetrators of the crime!

While catching criminals with blood-red hands—from killing animals or, at times, people—was the literal meaning, the term now generally applies to catching people in any act of wrongdoing. It does not have to be a criminal offence involving blood. It could be a tamer misdemeanour such as nicking an apple through the neighbour's kitchen window.

Here is how you can use the idiom in a sentence:

'The student was caught red-handed copying answers during the exam.'

'They were caught red-handed dumping trash in the river and fined heavily.'
'The hacker was caught red-handed accessing confidential files on the company server.'

The term 'red hand' was first used in 1432 in the Scottish Acts of Parliament of King James—who managed to rule two sovereign countries, Scotland and England, simultaneously, despite the fact that there was a bitter history of war between them. It is not known if English people felt that the Scottish king had stolen their royal crown. The 'red hand' most likely referred to someone illegally hunting game in a no-hunting zone.

Besides these two countries, King James also ruled Ireland. One of its provinces, Ulster, used the red hand as a heraldic symbol. A myth about its origin is that there was a boat race in which the first to touch the shore was to become the ruler. A contender cut off his own hand and threw it on the shore to claim the title. This myth was put forth by some as the origin of the 'red-handed' phrase, but it has largely been rejected in favour of the more literal explanation of the bloodied hands of killers.

'Caught rapid' or 'snared rapid' are variations of 'caught red-handed'. These terms, though, are of Irish origin. *In flagrante delicto* is the Latin version of the phrase. It can be literally translated as 'in blazing crime' and has the sense of catching someone in the heat of crime. Colloquially, the Latin phrase is used to refer to catching someone in the act of sexual misconduct—so use it with care.

'Red hand' became 'red-handed' in *Ivanhoe*, written by Sir Walter Scott in 1819. This influential historical novel is named after its protagonist Wilfred of Ivanhoe. With its fanciful descriptions of life in medieval England, it is credited with raising interest in romance and medievalism. Its large cast of characters features folk hero Robin Hood, the golden-hearted robber who stole from the rich and gave to the poor. Robin Hood protected the poor even when they were literally caught red-handed for poaching animals—because they were starving and needed the meat to survive.

This is the line of the novel in which 'red handed' appears: 'I did but tie one fellow, who was taken red-handed and in the fact, to the horns of a wild stag...' Besides being a writer, Scott was also a lawyer and a judge, so he would have had professional experience with red-handed criminals.

Phrases similar to 'caught red-handed' appear in many Scottish documents of the sixteenth and seventeenth centuries. The idiomatic usage of the phrase is found for the first time in George Alfred Lawrence's 1857 book *Guy Livingstone*:

> My companion picked up the object; and we had just time to make out that it was a bell-handle and name-plate, when the pursuers came up—six or seven "peelers" and specials, with a ruck of men and boys. We were collared on the instant. The fact of the property being found in our possessions constituted a *flagrans delictum*—we were caught red-handed.

Flagrans delictum, related to the Latin phrase 'in flagrante delicto', means a 'flagrant offence'.

George Alfred Lawrence was a British novelist who published *Guy Livingstone*, his first novel, anonymously. It met with success and launched the *beau sabreur* hero in English fiction. 'Beau sabreur' literally means 'handsome swordsman' in French. Used to describe dashing adventurers, the term was first applied as a nickname to Napoleon's brother-in-law Joachim Murat—who was also known, thanks to his flamboyant dressing style, as the Dandy King.

But that's a whole other story.

34

Blue blood

W.S. Gilbert (1836–1911), the celebrated English dramatist, librettist, poet and illustrator, was known to take potshots at the aristocracy. In the comic opera *Iolanthe*, the fairy Iolanthe has been banished from Fairyland for marrying a mortal. Her half-mortal son has grown up into the handsome shepherd Strephon. He is in love with the high-born beauty Phyllis. Her legal guardian, the Lord Chancellor, disapproves of this match—partly because of Strephon's low social status, but also because he himself as well as half the members of the House of Lords want to marry her. Phyllis rejects the aristocrats—who are portrayed as dim-witted, useless and privileged—in favour of the poor but virtuous Strephon. The peers beg her not to reject them simply because of their 'blue blood':

> Spurn not the nobly born
> With love affected,
> Nor treat with virtuous scorn
> The well connected.
> High rank involves no shame—
> We boast an equal claim
> With him of humble name
> To be respected!
> Blue blood! Blue blood!
> When virtuous love is sought,
> Thy power is naught,

Though dating from the Flood,
Blue blood!

As can be deciphered from this anecdote, blue blood is a term that refers to royalty, nobility or aristocracy. The Flood is a reference to the biblical story in which the old, corrupt world is destroyed by a flood, and only those aboard Noah's ark survive. Gilbert's aristocrats trace their ancestry back to that ark—like American aristocrats trace their roots to the Mayflower.

This is how you would use 'blue blood' in the modern world:

> 'The resume boasted blue blood, but the interview revealed a royal sense of entitlement and not much else.'
> 'Raghavendra thought his blue blood would open doors, but the biometric scanner only responds to keycards and competence.'
> 'His blue blood got him the corner office; her brilliance made him redundant by lunchtime.'

Now back to its roots: it is generally believed that the term blue blood is a direct translation of the Spanish *sangre azul*, a racist concept of the purity of blood. After centuries of Moorish rule, the nobility of Spain—who claimed ancestry from the Visigoths—wished to establish that their blood was not 'tainted' with that of the Moors or the Jews. This seems quite strange, as these communities took Spanish civilization and culture to new heights.

The Spaniards' blue blood was 'proven' by the blue veins that were visible through their fair skin. Since veins cannot be seen through the darker skin of the Moors and the Jews, this made the white nobles feel superior.

The English royalty borrowed this concept from their Spanish cousins. It was unfashionable to have a tan back then as it was associated with peasants who had to toil outdoors. The nobility, who did not have to labour under the sun, kept their skin untanned, allowing the blue veins to be seen.

Most members of European royal families—who are closely related through intermarriage—have the rare Rhesus Factor Negative or Rh-negative type of blood. It was speculated that Rh-negative blood has a high level of copper in it—giving it a markedly bluer tinge. According to this theory, European royalty would literally be blue-blooded. However, this theory has no scientific backing.

Another theory is that wealthy aristocrats were the only ones who could afford to eat with silverware and drink wine from silver goblets. They ingested trace amounts of silver with their food and drink, leading to a condition called argyria, which turns your skin a purplish-blue shade and gives you pronounced blue veins and arteries. This theory too is discredited.

The phrase was introduced into English by the 1830s. In 1834, a novel titled *Helen* written by the children's writer Maria Edgeworth mentions a person 'from Spain, of high rank and birth, of the sangre azul, the blue blood.' The term became common by the 1880s, when novelist Anthony Trollope used it in *The Duke's Children*: 'It is a point of conscience among the [...] one thousand of bluest blood [...] that everybody should know who everybody is. [...] It is a knowledge which the possession of the blue blood itself produces. There are countries with bluer blood than our own in which to be without such knowledge is a crime.'

Does the idea of blue-blooded privilege have a place in today's world where we are taught to judge people by merit and not the privilege of birth? While English dramatist W.S. Gilbert put across his opinion in a tongue-in-cheek manner in his comic operas, American historian and writer A.E. Samaan is blunter:

'This whole "blue blood" thing is gross and disgusting. The Royals are the original "supremacists" in believing themselves to be apart and above others.'

35

Cost an arm and a leg

'A reckless young pirate named Greg
Drank whisky straight out of a keg.
He cried "Look at me!"
In shark-ridden sea;
That drink cost an arm and a leg!'

—'The Boozy Buccaneer', Wendy Watson

Modern-day pirates probably do not wear eye-patches or have peg-legs, and are more likely to be seen sailing the virtual seas of the internet, where they get up to all sorts of nefarious activities. These include mischief-making—not for profit but for perverse pleasure.

One such pirate sent out an email in the year 2000. This was not one of those emails asking you to deposit money in a Nigerian bank account; it was a free history lesson. Its specific subject was the origins of words and phrases from the seventeenth century. Here is a paragraph from the email:

> In George Washington's days, there were no cameras. One's image was either sculpted or painted. Some paintings of Washington showed him standing behind a desk with one arm behind his back while others showed both legs and both arms. Prices charged by painters were not based on how many people were to be painted, but

by how many limbs were to be painted. Arms and legs are "limbs" therefore painting them would cost the buyer more. Hence the expression, "Okay, but it'll cost you an arm and a leg".

The good things in life are never free—it turns out that this free lesson in etymology does not, to use another limb-related phrase, have a leg to stand on. It is but a naughty bit of fabrication.

'An arm and a leg' means 'an exorbitant sum of money to pay for something'. Another way of expressing it is 'a king's ransom'. The latter phrase originally referred to the large sum of money that would have to be paid to free a king if he had been captured as a prisoner of war.

The exact origin of 'an arm and a leg' has not been established, though we know it to be coined in America after World War II. Its first documented usage in the figurative sense is found in the *Long Beach Independent* of December 1949: 'Food Editor Beulah Karney has more than 10 ideas for the homemaker who wants to say "Merry Christmas" and not have it cost her an arm and a leg.'

There are older phrases about paying a high price that mention either an arm or a leg, which may have influenced the coining of the combined phrase. The phrase 'I would give my right arm' dates back to the eighteenth century, if not earlier. It is used, for example, in *The Lady's Magazine: Or Entertaining Companion for the Fair Sex, Appropriated Solely to Their Use and Amusement* (1790): 'This is my sole desire—my only passion; and in order to gratify it, I would give my right arm, and my entire fortune.'

'If it takes a leg' was another expression in use in the nineteenth century. Here is an example of its use from a July

1875 issue of the Iowa newspaper *Burlington Daily Hawk-Eye*: 'A man who owes five years subscription to the Gazette is trying to stop his paper without paying up, and the editor is going to grab that back pay if it takes a leg.'

The literal use of 'an arm and a leg' dates back to the post-American Civil War era. Pensions were declared for soldiers who had paid the high price of losing both an upper and lower limb. So, it may have remained latent in American vocabulary from then and resurfaced after World War II when, once again, many a soldier lost an arm and a leg—thus turning it into a metaphor for a high price to pay.

In the case of the whiskey-chugging pirate Greg in the limerick at the beginning of the chapter, it is not apparent whether the 'arm and a leg' the keg of whiskey cost him were figurative or literal. A keg of whiskey would have cost him a lot of money to buy, not to mention the hangover with which he would have had to pay for it. There is also the distinct possibility that, with so much liquor in his system, he lost his balance and fell into the shark-infested sea.

Here's how you can use the idiom in your everyday conversations:

> 'The Coldplay concert ticket cost an arm and a leg, but hearing them live gave me chills worth every penny.'
> 'These designer outfits cost an arm and a leg—I'll stick to my T-shirt and jeans, thank you!'
> 'The new iPhone looks great, but I'm not paying an arm and a leg just for a slightly better camera.'

36
An apple a day keeps the doctor away

Or does it? There is a 2015 study that finds no evidence to support the apple aphorism—people who eat this fruit, it turns out, do not consult the doctor less often. I do not eat apples myself, as I follow a low carbohydrate diet. Proponents of this diet say that sugar—natural or otherwise—is the root of all evil. Apples contain fructose, a form of sugar, and therefore fall in the forbidden category.

Apples originally meant any round fruit from a tree. We think of the biblical forbidden fruit of Adam and Eve as being an apple, but in the King James Bible of 1611, it is referred to simply as a fruit—which makes perfect sense to devotees of the low carbohydrate diet for whom virtually all fruit is forbidden. (If that sounds unhealthy to you, do note that the diet recommends substituting fruit with vegetables—which can provide you with the nutrients present in fruit, minus the sugar.)

The irony is that the apple idiom is one of the few that hail from Wales, my birthplace. Well, not exactly in the form that we know the saying today, but definitely in its essence: 'A Pembrokeshire proverb. Eat an apple on going to bed, And you'll keep the doctor from earning his bread.' This is from *Notes and Queries* magazine, February 1866. Pembrokeshire is a county in the southwest of Wales.

The modern version of the saying—an apple a day keeps

the doctor away—likely first appeared in the *South Wales Daily News* on 18 February 1892. The author, under the pen name Cosmos, wrote:

> Now that fruit is so cheap, I wonder it is not seen on every breakfast table. The morning is the time for its consumption... The old proverb has it—
> An apple a day
> Keeps the doctor away.
> And to begin the day with fruit has a beneficial effect on our constitutions.

There have been many variants of the phrase. A few from the West Country of England are recorded in *The Youth's Companion* (Boston, USA) of 10 August 1899. From these versions of the saying, it appears that some people were not satisfied with just one apple a day. Robust red-cheeked health was promised with increased consumption:

> Three each day, sev'n days a week
> Ruddy apple, ruddy cheek.

Another version seems to be composed by someone who had something against the medical profession:

> Apple in the morning,
> Doctor's warning.
>
> Roast apple at night
> Starved the doctor outright.
>
> Eat an apple going to bed.
> Knocked the doctor on the head.

I am guessing this rhyme was not popular with the medical fraternity.

Interestingly, its first two verses are reminiscent of a Mother Goose rhyme I learnt as a child:

A red sky in the morning is the shepherd's warning
A red sky at night is the shepherd's delight.

A long-standing humorous twist to the idiom references the breath-taking effect of onions: 'An apple a day keeps the doctor away, but an onion a day keeps everyone away.'

With all this talk about its health benefits, I do feel the pressure to give in and consume an apple. And I have found the perfect form in which to indulge in it: apple cider vinegar diluted in water, which has long been believed to possess multiple health benefits.

Based on personal experience, I have updated the proverb: 'Apple cider vinegar every day, keeps your medical problems at bay.'

37

Play it by ear

'I want to be an honest man and I want to be a good writer. And I don't know if one ever gets to be what one wants to be. You just have to play it by ear and pray for rain.'

—James Baldwin (1924–87)

James Baldwin was an African-American writer who grew up in a dirt-poor family in New York. Racism, poverty and domestic abuse were some of the obstacles he faced in getting an education. And yet he managed to write a play at school that was directed by his teacher. This started him off on a journey of prolific and brilliant writing. Be it in his life or his writing, it could be said that Baldwin played it by ear. As in, he improvised: the odds were stacked against him, but he made the most of each obstacle that cropped up in his path with his writing.

'Playing it by ear' means to act as per the demands of a situation rather than on the basis of a plan. Baldwin believed that the latter was futile as you never know what life is going to throw at you. This is echoed in the lyrics of musician John Lennon: 'Life is what happens to you while you're busy making other plans.'

The literal meaning of playing it by ear comes from music. It is when you play a tune not by reading sheet music but by listening and intuitively following the melody. It is interesting that playing it by ear has come to mean improvisation because in the original sense, you were not necessarily improvising: you could be playing a piece of music exactly as it had been composed, even if you were not reading the notation.

'By ear' actually refers not to the ear itself but what you do with it—listen. This is called metonymy: when you use a word to refer to something closely related to it. As when Shakespeare wrote in Julius Caesar, 'Friends, Romans, countrymen, lend me your ears,' Antony was not asking people to cut off their ears for him, but to listen to him. Similarly, 'having a good ear for music' means the ability to perceive musical qualities such as pitch and timbre and to appreciate the finer points of musical compositions. People with a good ear for music can often reproduce a piece of music they have heard only once. In other words, they can play that piece by ear.

The earliest known use of the word 'ear' in the sense of musical ability is by the monk William Bonde in 1526. In his treatise on English called *Pylgrimage of Perfection*, he wrote: 'In the psalmody ... haue a good eare.' Psalmody simply means the singing of psalms. It was important to have a good ear for music if one were to sing religious songs properly.

The sense of playing without reading music is found a century later in 1658—in John Playford's *A Brief Introduction to the Skill of Musick*. The *Oxford English Dictionary* cites it as the first to use the phrase, with the following definition: 'to learn to play by rote or ear without book'.

It is not until 1839 that we find the idiomatic use of playing by ear even being hinted at. It is in the review of a book called *Deerbrook* by Harriet Martineau in the *Edinburgh Review*: 'Miss Austen is like one who plays by ear, while Miss Martineau understands the science. Miss Austen has the air of being led to right conclusions by an intuitive tact—Miss Martineau unfolds her knowledge of the principles on which her correct judgment is founded.'

It was only in the twentieth century that we see the phrase being used in the sense that we use it today. It appears in the novel *The Twisted Claw* (1939), from the famous Hardy Boys series by Franklin W. Dixon, when the two characters Frank and Joe are locked in a dark storeroom: '"I guess we'll just have to wait until someone comes down again, and then play it by ear," Joe muttered.'

I used to be part of an improv theatre group. 'Improv' is short for 'improvisation'. And that is precisely what this type of performance is all about. You ask the audience to suggest an idea and you build a theatrical—often comical—scene out of it. It is the height of being spontaneous. Your dialogues are ad lib. Your actions are impromptu. And yet you have to be mindful of building a coherent scene with your co-actors that will entertain the audience. Improv truly teaches you to turn playing it by ear into an art. It is probably what we end up doing unconsciously in life too. And that is probably what Baldwin was talking about: with practice, you get so good at playing it by ear that, once in a while, you achieve a state of grace—and a little of the much-prayed-for rain falls blissfully in your life.

38

Bite the bullet

Have you ever forced yourself to do something that you dreaded doing? Perhaps because that difficult thing was something that simply *had* to be done? That's called biting the bullet.

Maybe you had to wade through murky water to get home when the city got flooded during the monsoons. You were scared of the dangers that lurked in the water—potholes, bacteria, or worse. But the water showed no signs of receding, so you bit the bullet and took the plunge. Or maybe you were scared of showing your report card to your dad but you plucked up the courage to do it. You bit the bullet and faced your father's wrath. Or maybe you were hesitant to take the Covid vaccine, but you decided to bite the bullet.

Where did this phrase originate? Did it start out with people literally biting a bullet for some reason? If so, it seems logical that it would be people in the army doing the biting, given their direct association with guns and ammunition.

Well, one theory is that the phrase originated during India's Sepoy Mutiny of 1857.

A new type of rifle had been issued to the sepoys, the Indian soldiers in the British army, which used greased paper cartridges that had to be bitten to release the powder. It was suspected that the cartridges were greased with beef or pork fat—which made it unacceptable to both Hindu and Muslim soldiers. The theory is that the phrase came about due to British officers insisting that the sepoys put aside their religious concerns and 'bite the bullet'. This led to a rebellion that shook the British Raj—to the extent that the Sepoy Mutiny is also known as India's First War of Independence.

Another theory is that patients, often soldiers wounded in combat, literally bit the bullet when amputations or other surgeries were being performed on them without anaesthesia—to take their mind off the pain and help them avoid screaming or biting their tongue off.

But both the Sepoy Mutiny and the surgery-related theories have been discredited.

The accepted theory is that soldiers used to bite a bullet when being punished by flogging. They did this to control their urge to scream—because it was a matter of honour not to do so. The following is an entry from Francis Grose's *A Classical Dictionary of the Vulgar Tongue* (1785): 'Nightingale. A soldier who, as the term is, sings out at the halberts. It is a point of honour in some regiments, among the grenadiers, never to cry out, or become nightingales, whilst under the discipline of the cat of nine tails; to avoid which, they chew a bullet.'

So, you bit a bullet to avoid 'singing like a nightingale'—a euphemistic way of saying 'crying out' or 'screaming'.

While the flogging-related theory is probably the most accurate one, the theories of the idiom originating in surgeries performed without anaesthesia or in the Sepoy Mutiny are certainly more dramatic.

The first documented figurative use of the phrase is by Nobel Prize-winning English writer Rudyard Kipling in his 1891 novel *The Light That Failed*. This semi-autobiographical novel is about an artist called Dick Heldar, who goes blind. Let me quote the relevant bit: '"Steady, Dickie, steady!" said the deep voice in his ear, and the grip tightened. "Bite on the bullet, old man, and don't let them think you're afraid."'

As you can see, the phrase was used in the sense of showing courage. As an aside, it is interesting to note that while this novel was poorly received by critics when it was first published, it is still in print today, 135 years later.

So that's the second connection the 'bite the bullet' phrase has with India—and this time it's a true one, for Rudyard Kipling was born in this country.

Before moving on, a last quote. One in which the idiom is worded exactly as we use it today. This is from P.G. Wodehouse, the British humorist known for creating unforgettable characters like Bertie Wooster and Jeeves. In his 1923 novel, *The Inimitable Jeeves*, Bertie Wooster says to Jeeves, 'Brace up and bite the bullet. I'm afraid I've bad news for you.'

39

Crocodile tears

'As when a weary Traveller, that strays
[...]
Doth meet a cruel crafty Crocodile,
Which in false Grief hiding his harmful Guile,
Doth weep full sore, and sheddeth tender Tears:
The foolish Man, that pities all this while
His mournful Plight, is swallow'd up unwares...'

— *The Faerie Queene*, Edmund Spenser, 1590

Crocodiles have been around for a long, long time. We know that they first appeared over 200 million years ago in the Mesozoic Era, aka the age of dinosaurs! What is not known, however, is whether crocodiles shed tears when their prehistoric cousins, the dinosaurs, went extinct about 65 million years ago.

Crocodiles are believed to cry when devouring their prey. This has given rise to the phrase 'crocodile tears', meaning fake sadness. Crocodile tears are shed by insincere or hypocritical people. They pretend to be sad about something that they are secretly happy about.

Crocs are ruthless carnivores. Crying over the human or animal they kill to eat seems fake. Yet their tears are real; unlike, for example, the 'crocodile tears' politicians are known to shed over the despicable living conditions of slum dwellers.

What the reptile does have in common with the politicians, though, is that the tears do not come from real emotion.

An absence of emotion, however, does not make the tears fake. You see, the process of eating activates a crocodile's tear glands. This happens especially when they have their meal on dry land. If you get close to crocodiles while they are dining on a beach—something I do not recommend—you will hear them hissing and huffing. They blow warm air through their sinuses while they chew to stimulate their tear glands. It helps them keep their eyes lubricated while they are not in water. Similarly, humans shed tears when they get sand in their eyes: it is the body's way of protecting the organ. It would be wrong to call those fake tears as it *is* the physical act of crying. Same is the case with crocodiles.

Nevertheless, for hundreds of years, people have used the words 'crocodile tears' to refer to a pretence of sorrow. The earliest record of this idea is in the proverbs attributed to Greek writer Plutarch who lived c. 46–120 CE. These proverbs speak of people who lament someone's death though they secretly wished for or even caused it.

The first known English reference is in *The Voyage and Travail of Sir John Maundeville*, c. 1400: 'These serpents slay men; and they eat them weeping.' This notion also became associated with the Christian concept of false repentance, akin to Judas's tears after betraying Jesus.

Shakespeare wrote about crocodile tears in various plays. In *Othello*, the protagonist believes that his wife is being unfaithful to him. He says:

> If that the earth could teem with woman's tears,
> Each drop she falls would prove a crocodile.
>
> (Act 4, Scene 1)

Shakespeare's contemporary, Edmund Spenser, quoted at the beginning of this chapter, wrote about crocodile tears in *The Faerie Queene*, one of the longest poems written in the English language.

The first purely figurative use of crocodile tears to imply insincerity is from the sixteenth century: Edmund Grindal, archbishop of York and Canterbury, wrote in 1563: 'I begin to fear, lest his humility ... be a counterfeit humility, and his tears crocodile tears.' Then, in *Dido and Aeneas*, the 1688 opera by Henry Purcell, we come across it again. When Aeneas abandons Dido with melodramatic justifications, she says:

> Thus on the fatal banks of Nile,
> Weeps the deceitful crocodile.

The lachrymose crocodile was thought by many to be a myth for several centuries. Nobody in living memory had actually *seen* the reptile's tears. That is, until scientists in Florida decided to carry out an experiment in 2006—though the subjects were not crocodiles but their close cousins, the caimans. Apparently, it was easier to study them feeding on land at St. Augustine Alligator Farm Zoological Park.

Five of the seven feeding animals were observed to weep while eating, taking crocodile tears from the realm of myth to reality.

40
Cat got your tongue?

The question is posed to a person who is being unusually quiet—from guilt, fear, embarrassment or just not knowing what to say.

When Mom finds a box of sweets unexpectedly empty, she might question her kid about it. And if he doesn't answer, she might ask him, 'Has the cat got your tongue?' Of course, this question could be posed to Dad as well. It's not always the kid who remains silent after being naughty!

Let me tell you about an interesting medical case: some years ago, a 69-year-old lady developed a painfully swollen tongue that made her speechless. After various tests, her doctor detected a *Pasteurella multocida* infection, which is caused by dog or—you guessed it—cat bites. And the dear old lady had a pet cat, making this the first reported medical case in which a cat *literally* got someone's tongue.

Perhaps a similar case long ago led to the coining of the phrase 'cat got your tongue'? The more popular theory, however, is that the cat in the idiom is not a cat at all, but a whip.

The cat o' nine tails is a many-tailed whip often referred to in short as 'the cat'. It was used for flogging sailors as formal punishment by the British Royal Navy.

The cat was usually made up of nine knotted cotton cords, though it could also be made of leather and tipped with metal barbs. It was designed to lacerate the skin—and it was possibly called a cat because the lacerations reminded people of cat scratches.

Though, unlike a cat's scratches, the whipping caused so much pain that the sailor would be silenced from passing out; sometimes even permanently, when the flogging killed him.

Two other explanations of the idiom 'cat got your tongue' involve actual cats, though ones imbued with magical or divine powers.

Cats had divine status in ancient Egypt. If someone lied, committed blasphemy or criticized the rulers, their tongues were cut off and fed to these godly cats. Food for thought for anyone thinking of committing similar crimes.

The second explanation comes from the Middle Ages, when Christians feared witches, their black cats and their curses. Apparently, if you spied on a witch, her cat would use black magic to steal your tongue, so that you could not report what you had seen.

An old French idiom, *je donne ma langue au chat*, literally means 'I give my tongue to the cat'. It is used in the way we say 'I give up' when asked a riddle we don't know the answer to. This French phrase could also be the precursor to the English one.

The oldest example of 'cat got your tongue' in print is from a write-up in the December 1859 issue of an American newspaper, *The Racine Democrat*. It narrates an incident in which a certain person does not respond to another, and the latter remarks, 'Oh ho! The cat got your tongue has it?'

I, on the other hand, talk so much that I would never get asked this question.

41
Get your goat

I once kidnapped a kid.

I myself was a child then. While on vacation in the countryside, my brother and I found the kid wandering around alone and, on a whim, brought him back to the house we were staying at. We had a marvellous time playing with him—away from adult eyes, of course—until we heard a commotion outside. The irate villagers had traced their missing baby goat to our place.

We had got their goat—in both the literal and figurative senses of the word. We had taken their kid goat and, understandably, angered them in the process. We sheepishly returned their property and waited for the inevitable punishment from our parents.

The phrase 'to get someone's goat', meaning 'to annoy or anger someone', dates back to the early 1900s. And one theory about its origin is linked to the kidnapping of goats. These animals were kept in the stables of skittish thoroughbreds to keep the latter calm. Unscrupulous rivals would 'get the goat'— or steal it—the night before a race so the horse would be out of sorts and perform badly. Beyond the practical purpose these goats may have served, horse-racers believed their presence brought good luck. And, as early as 1912, the phrase about getting one's goat was thought to be linked to these mascot goats in racehorse stables: a 1912 issue of *Country Life* reports, 'The origin of this rather cumbrous jest appears to lie in the fact that a goat was considered a mascot in racing stables, so that to lose your goat was one of the most dreadful things that could befall you.'

The earliest use of 'goat' as slang for anger is in the 1904 book *Life in Sing Sing* by Number 1500. Prisoner number 1500 describes life behind bars in the notorious New York prison called Sing Sing. The harsh conditions in this jail could certainly get one's goat, its sing-song name notwithstanding. Sing Sing comes from Sintsink, the name of the Native American tribe from whom the land on which the prison stands was originally bought. Incidentally, the American slang 'up the river', meaning 'imprisonment', comes from the fact that convicts were sent up the Hudson River from New York City to this prison.

Why 'goat' should mean anger is not clear, though it may have something to do with the fact that Satan is depicted with the cloven hooves of a goat. Getting your goat could amount to bringing out the devil in you in the form of anger.

Though 'goat' signifying anger appears in *Life in Sing Sing*, 'get your goat' does not. The earliest example of the idiom that one knows of is in a story about the US Navy called 'Papeeyon' by Stephen French Whitman, published in *Collier's* magazine on 28 October 1905:

> "[...] You were there, too, then? You were ashore?"
> "Ha! Ha!" He slapped Patrick on the shoulder and lay back grinning at me. "If that don't get my goat."

A second example appeared just days later, on 18 November 1905, in a *Washington Times* report on a boxing match between two sailors, one British and the other American. 'John Bull took another fall out of Uncle Sam last night [...] I think the crowd got his goat, or the idea of fighting—one or the other—because he did not say boo and sat down like a mope.'

The French phrase *prendre le chevre*—literally 'to take the goat'—also means to lose one's temper. It dates back to the early seventeenth century and the possibility exists that the English phrase is adapted from it—though it has not been corroborated.

The year 1908 was when the expression entered the mainstream. In June that year, the song 'Somebody's Got Your Goat' came out:

> Somebody's got my goat...
> He's lost, strayed or stolen
> When he began to feel his oats
> He went out chasing nannie goats
> You never struck such a giddy old buck
> Has anybody seen my goat?

A few days later, an article in the *New-York Tribune* identified the expression as Navy slang.

Goats were considered lucky not just by horse trainers but by sailors as well. You would find them aboard many a ship. A goat has been the mascot of the United States Naval Academy since at least 1893. According to a *New-York Tribune* article from that year, when a football match took place between the navy and the army in Annapolis, the navy took a black billy goat called El Cid along—and credited their win to its presence.

When you consider that some of the earliest examples of the idiom in use are in the context of the navy—predating horse-racing references—and that goats were an established mascot of the navy, the theory that 'get your goat' originated in naval slang seems to be the more convincing one.

42

Break a leg

Are you superstitious? Many people are. Even those of us who think of ourselves as rational people end up quietly complying with certain superstitions 'just in case'.

Many superstitions are unique to particular sections of people. Amongst stage actors, for example, it is considered bad luck to whistle in the theatre, to say the last line of a play during rehearsals, or to mention Shakespeare's *Macbeth* in the green room. There is a fourth superstition as well: it is thought to bring bad luck to wish someone good luck before a performance. This may stem from the old belief that there are mischievous sprites about who make the opposite of what is being wished for come true. Wish for something bad, and good will happen. 'Break a leg' is the 'negative' wish of choice in the world of theatre.

I myself have dabbled in drama and was surprised when, just before my debut public performance, my heroine whispered 'break a leg' to me. I was already nervous. This made me go over the edge. I mean this figuratively, of course. If I had gone over the edge of the stage, I may have actually broken my leg.

In 1921, Robert Wilson Lynd published 'A Defence of Superstition' in *The New Statesman*, a British magazine. Lynd believed that the theatre was the second-most superstitious institution in England, next only to horse racing. Since wishing someone luck in horse racing was considered unlucky, Lynd said, 'You should say something insulting such as, "May you break your leg!"' However, while Lynd did mention the superstitious nature of theatre as an institution, he did not specifically connect 'break a leg' to it.

The first record of the phrase in the context of theatre is from 1939. In her autobiography, *A Peculiar Treasure*, Edna Ferber mentions '...the understudies sitting in the back row politely wishing the various principals would break a leg.' This, of course, is about literally wishing that an actor would break a leg, so the understudy could get a chance to be on stage.

In the 1948 edition of Bernard Sobel's *The Theatre Handbook and Digest of Plays*, he writes about theatrical superstitions: '...before a performance actors never wish each other good luck, but say "I hope you break a leg."' The same year, an American newspaper, *The Charleston Gazette*, in its 'Ask the Gazette' column, mentions the superstition of wishing actors that they break a leg to avoid bad luck. These were the first mentions in print of the superstitious use of the phrase in theatre.

There is an old German phrase—*Hals- und Beinbruch*—which means 'neck and bone fracture' that was popular in the German Air Force. It was used in a way similar to 'break a leg'. It may have been a corruption of an old Hebrew phrase *hatzlakha u-brakha*, which means success and blessing (and sounds a bit like a jumbled version of 'break a leg'). Many Jews migrated from Germany to America. Some of them became a part of the theatre scene and could have introduced 'break a leg' as a light-hearted twist to the German-Jewish originals.

Another theory about the origin of the phrase is that it is an old-fashioned way of referring to bending your knee to curtsy. When people said 'break a leg' to you, they were wishing that you got an ovation at the end of your performance so you would have to bow in acknowledgement. A variation on this theory is that people threw coins on stage if they enjoyed the show and you had to bend to pick up the money. Yet another variation has to do with the handle of the crank used for lowering and raising the curtain being called a leg. If the show was a hit, there were many curtain calls. And the strain on this 'leg' could break it.

In vaudeville theatre in the US, many performers were signed on but not all of them made it to the stage. Only those who did got paid. They had to cross the line from the wings to the stage to qualify for payment. This was known as the 'leg line'. If you crossed—or broke—it, you were in luck. This is one more possible explanation for why people wished performers thus.

As a phrase, 'break a leg' existed well before the twentieth century, but it had a different meaning. Around the year 1670, if you told someone to break a leg, you would be insulting the person, because it meant 'give birth to a bastard'. The theatrical phrase obviously has no connection with this older, less pleasant usage.

There is no definitive conclusion about the etymology of 'break a leg'. But the many colourful theories about it more than make up for the lack of certainty. It has travelled beyond theatre to other professions and has become something of an exhortation to put energy into making something a success. At the moment, I am wishing that I 'break a leg' as I endeavour to complete this book.

43
Barking up the wrong tree

If you asked me to answer a question about Java programming, you would be barking up the wrong tree, as coding is not my area of expertise.

We take steps hoping to get a particular result, but sometimes it turns out to be the wrong course of action. We end up misdirecting our efforts on the basis of a wrong choice or assumption. For example, we could be asking the wrong person for something—that person may not be in a position to, or may not want to, give us what we want. Wasting our energies and time pursuing the wrong person, thing or approach is known as barking up the wrong tree.

I came across a book the other day called *Barking Up the Wrong Tree*. It is written by Eric Barker—yes, that is his name. He claims the book can teach you how to succeed in life. The premise is that the advice we have been given on how to achieve success, though seemingly logical, is wrong; hence the title. The author says that the best people to learn cooperation from are pirates and serial killers, that Genghis Khan can teach you about work–life balance, and that topping your class is not the best marker for success. So, Barker says, if you worked hard to top your class—as advised by your parents—you were barking up the wrong tree. Hm.

With all this barking, there must be a dog somewhere, right? Yes. It turns out that the phrase originated in the sport of raccoon hunting that was popular in 1820s' USA. Raccoons, nocturnal mammals native to North America, were usually hunted on moonlit nights with the help of dogs trained to follow their scent. The sport was popularly known as coon hunting and the dogs used for the purpose were called coonhounds or coon dogs.

The hounds that were imported into North America in the colonial period were good for fox hunting because foxes hid closer to the ground. Raccoons would take refuge high up in a tree and the hounds would lose their scent. The hounds' job was to go to the tree in which a raccoon was hiding and bark to let the hunter know its whereabouts. Sometimes, the hound would get the tree wrong because the raccoon had either climbed up a different one or indeed climbed that particular tree but then jumped to another one. Whatever the reason, the dog would often end up barking up the wrong tree, misleading the hunter.

This led to hunters and breeders selectively breeding hounds with a stronger sense of smell—these came to be known as coon dogs. They, presumably, never barked up the wrong tree!

The phrase applied to the hunting not just of raccoons but also of other creatures. A dictionary called *Americanisms—Old & New* was published in 1889. Its author, John S. Farmer, explains: '... supposing they had "treed" their game when in reality, especially in the case of opossums and squirrels and such-like animals, it had escaped [...]. The dogs consequently were left barking up the wrong tree.'

The phrase appeared in American newspapers throughout the 1830s. This is an example from *The Adams Sentinel*, March 1834: 'Gineral you are barkin' up the wrong tree this time, for I jest see that rackoon jump to the next tree, and afore this he is a mile off in the woods.'

An earlier record of the phrase in use is from the 1833 book, *Sketches and Eccentricities of Col. David Crockett, of West Tennessee*. Attributed to James Strange French, this book is about

David 'Davy' Crockett (1786–1836), a soldier and politician who became an American folk hero. The book describes Crockett's reaction to one of his opponents thus: 'I told him that he had got hold of the wrong man; that he didn't know who he was fooling with; that he reminded me of the meanest thing on God's earth, an old coon dog barking up the wrong tree.'

The phrase grew in popularity especially in the 1940s, when it was used in detective fiction while talking about investigating suspects who turned out to be innocent or pursuing leads that turned out to be false. But the earliest example of the phrase in print is in James Kirke Paulding's *Westward Ho!* published in 1832:

> Here he made a note in his book, and I begun to smoke him for one of those fellows that drive a sort of a trade of making books about old Kentuck and the western country: so I thought I'd set him barking up the wrong tree a little, and I told him some stories that were enough to set the Mississippi a-fire; but he put them all down in his book.

I like this example for three reasons. One, of course, is that it is the oldest known use of the phrase. Two, because of the naughtiness of the narrator, who deliberately misleads the writer. And three, it is a lesson for writers like me, to use more than one source to confirm our facts!

44

Wolf in sheep's clothing

'Beware, beware, be skeptical
Of their smiles, their smiles of plated gold
Deceit so natural
But a wolf in sheep's clothing is more than a warning...
[...]
Karma's gonna come collect your debt'

These lines are from the lyrics of the song 'Wolf in Sheep's Clothing' by the band Set It Off. While the song was written in 2014 and is credited to Erik Ron, Cody Carson, Dan Clermont and Brandon Paddock, perhaps Jesus Christ should also have been included in the list of contributors. After all, in essence, the idea of a wolf in sheep's clothing finds its origin in the Bible: 'Beware of false prophets, which come to you in sheep's clothing, but inwardly they are ravening wolves.' (Matthew 7:15 KJV) In simple English, this means that looks can be deceptive: someone who appears to be good can be evil or dangerous. The next verse says 'by their fruits shall ye know them', meaning that their actions will ultimately reveal their true nature.

This theme from Jesus's sermon cropped up again and again in the following centuries, both in religious and secular works. It became so popular that a proverb was coined in Latin: *Pelle sub agnina latitat mens saepe lupina*, which can be translated as 'Under a sheep's skin often hides a wolfish mind'.

Some say that the sheepskin-clad wolf predates even the Bible—that it is one of Aesop's fables. But there is no actual record of the fable till the twelfth century. Aesop was a Greek slave from the sixth century BCE who became the world's most famous fabulist—but over the centuries many fables that he had not written were also attributed to him. So, whether this fable is genuinely his is unknown.

In George Fyler Townsend's 1867 version of Aesop's Fables, the story 'The Wolf in Sheep's Clothing' describes a wolf who disguises himself in sheepskin and infiltrates a flock to find easy prey. At night, he is shut in the fold along with the real sheep. Later, the shepherd returns to slaughter a sheep for his supper and, unknowingly, selects the disguised wolf. The first actual record of this construct is in the twelfth-century Greek work *Progymnasmata* by Nikephoros Basilakes. It is prefaced with the statement: 'You can get into trouble by wearing a disguise.'

The moral of this story is that life has a way of making you pay for your deceit. Or, as the Set It Off song puts it, 'Karma's gonna come collect your debt.' The concept of karma, now popular throughout the world, comes from the Hindu–Buddhist belief that your actions determine your fate.

Yet another rendition of the fable appears in the fifteenth-century work *Hecatomythium* by Italian professor Laurentius Abstemius. Here, the wolf in sheepskin is caught, killed and hanged from a tree as a lesson. Abstemius says in his comment on the story, 'many in sheep's clothing do the work of wolves'.

In his *Cento Favole Morali* (100 Moral Fables), sixteenth-century Italian poet Giovanni Maria Verdizotti introduces yet another variation on the tale. Here the wolf disguises itself as the shepherd and tries to imitate his call. This wakes the real shepherd and his dogs. Hampered by the sheepskin, the wolf cannot run fast enough and is killed. This is the version of the story that debuted in the English language in 1692 as 'The Wolf turn'd Shepherd' by Roger L'Estrange.

As an aside, I feel wolves have got a bad rap over the centuries. They have been portrayed as vicious, cunning animals in religious works, fables and folklore. In reality, they are shy and beautiful creatures. There is no denying that they are predators and hunt other animals for food, but they usually do not attack humans. In fact, because they have been hunted by humans over the centuries, they fear us. But the wolves in Northern Canada, for example, who rarely see humans, actually come and greet the biologists who arrive there by helicopter!

So, it is not the real wolves we need to fear. But, as so many have warned us, we do need to be wary of human wolves who disguise themselves as benign beings to prey on the unsuspecting.

45
Elementary, my dear Watson

'Elementary, my dear Watson'—this is one of the best-known phrases that Sherlock Holmes never said. At least, not the original Sherlock Holmes character in the series of stories written by Sir Arthur Conan Doyle. However, in movie adaptations of the books, the fictional detective does say it to his loyal assistant and friend Dr Watson after explaining the reasoning behind his amazing deductions.

The line was made famous by the movie *The Adventures of Sherlock Holmes*, released in 1939. Basil Rathbone, who played Holmes in this movie, was a celebrated actor of his time. After he said this line, it found a permanent place in popular culture. However, this was not the first time the sentence was spoken. It was heard earlier in the 1929 movie *The Return of Sherlock Holmes*, which was the first sound film about the detective. Actor Clive Brook, who played the detective in this version, used the phrase at the end of the movie.

Even before its use in movies, author P.G. Wodehouse used the phrase in his book *Psmith, Journalist*, published in 1915. 'Elementary, my dear Watson, elementary,' murmured Psmith in this story.

Holmes's brilliant deductions were way beyond the reasoning capabilities of his assistant Dr Watson. So, I think Holmes was being a little condescending when he described his complex reasoning as elementary to Watson.

If you've just impressed your friends with your astute

deductions about, say, what's really happening behind the scenes in politics, you could impress them further by adding, 'Elementary, my dear Watson.'

46

Green-eyed monster

'O beware, my lord, of jealousy;
It is the green-eyed monster which doth mock the meat
it feeds on.'

—*Othello*, Act 3, Scene 3

The character Iago says this to William Shakespeare's tragic hero Othello. The intention of Iago, supposedly Othello's trusted companion, is to sow doubt in Othello's mind about the faithfulness of his wife, Desdemona. The word 'doth' is an archaic form of the word 'does'.

In the play, Othello is a Moorish general of Venice. When he passes over Iago to appoint Cassio as his chief lieutenant, Iago plots to destroy Othello by falsely implicating Desdemona and Cassio in a love affair.

Shakespeare likened jealousy to a green-eyed monster in the aforementioned lines. Perhaps he was thinking of cats, many of which have green eyes and are known to toy with their prey before killing them, when he said the monster mocks the meat it feeds on.

The Bard was certainly not thinking of mock meat—a recent phenomenon that seems to have caught the world's fancy. I know this is a digression, but mock meats, also called meat analogues, are meat substitutes made with vegetarian ingredients. I wonder what Shakespeare would have made of it—he did write 'Anger's my meat; I will sup upon myself, / And so shall starve with feeding' in Act 4, Scene 2 of his play *Coriolanus*. In the tragedy, a mother who is angry because her son has been banished from Rome says these words. Perhaps her reaction approximates the reaction Shakespeare might have had if someone offered him mock meat.

The person who experiences jealousy can end up being consumed or destroyed by it. The person is 'meat for the monster'; hence the expression. In the case of the otherwise perfect Othello, jealousy was his major flaw that ended up consuming him.

But why is the monster green-eyed? Scholars suggest that green represents immaturity, like the green growth of a young plant. It is also the colour of a sickly complexion. Some people turn pale green with nausea. And sometimes with jealousy. But such assumptions are not convincing enough. In my view, cats are the only plausible explanation.

In Shakespeare's England, colours were often associated with emotions. Green, for example, was associated with envy and jealousy. And even today, it is. Some of the other contemporary colour associations are of red with anger, yellow with cowardice, purple with bravery—hence the Purple Heart, the American military honour—and blue with sadness.

Coming back to green, it is more common nowadays to say 'He is green with envy' rather than 'He is green with jealousy'. What is the difference between the two green emotions—envy and jealousy? I have often heard them being used interchangeably, but there are those who insist that they have distinct meanings.

Here's one way of differentiating between the two words: you can feel envy about something you want but do not have, but you feel jealousy over something that you have but fear you may lose. You may envy someone her wealth, high marks, high-profile job or good looks. You may experience jealousy if you suspect that you are losing your girlfriend to another man. You can be jealous of all her male friends if you are very insecure.

You can also be described as jealous when you are careful about guarding or keeping something you have—not necessarily your girl- or boyfriend. You could be jealous about your good reputation, for example. After all, you've worked hard to build it. You would not want to lose it. We all need to jealously guard the rights we have as citizens of a democracy—otherwise we may one day wake up to find that we do not live in a democracy anymore!

Let's come back to Shakespeare. *Othello*, which he wrote in 1604, was not the first play in which he used the green-eyed idiom. In *The Merchant of Venice*, which he wrote in 1596, the character Portia speaks thus:

> How all the other passions fleet to air,
> As doubtful thoughts, and rash-embraced despair,
> And shuddering fear, and green-eyed jealousy!
>
> (Act 3, Scene 2)

Some of us read *The Merchant of Venice* in school. In this play, the merchant Antonio takes a loan from Shylock to help his friend Bassanio court Portia. When Antonio is unable repay Shylock, the latter demands a pound of his flesh as per the terms of the loan. Portia, now the wife of Antonio's friend Bassanio, disguises herself as a lawyer—a male lawyer—and saves Antonio.

The lines I quoted are spoken by Portia in the scene where Bassanio has to choose one of three caskets, gold, silver or lead. As per Portia's father's will, he can marry her only if he picks the one which contains Portia's portrait. He picks the lead casket, which is the right one, and wins the lottery. Both he and Portia are overjoyed. In the lines I quoted, Portia describes how the intense love she feels for Bassanio overpowers negative emotions like jealousy and fear.

In *The Merchant of Venice*, Shakespeare described jealousy as merely being green-eyed. He had not yet made it a monster. By the time he wrote *Othello*, he had turned jealousy into the far more dramatic green-eyed monster that continues to enrich our language four centuries later!

It is ironic that Iago describes jealousy thus and warns Othello about it—because it is Iago's lie about Othello's wife having an affair that is the cause of Othello's jealousy. But I do like the words Shakespeare puts in Iago's mouth. A few lines after the 'green-eyed' reference, Iago describes a jealous person as one 'Who dotes, yet doubts, suspects, yet strongly loves!'

A wonderful description, isn't it, of a person who is in thrall to the green-eyed monster?

You can use the idiom in a sentence in the following ways:

'When Ashok saw his girlfriend talking to her ex-boyfriend, he let the green-eyed monster get the better of him.'
'As Sushma listened to the applause for her rival's performance, the green-eyed monster coiled tighter in her chest.'

47
Murphy's law

'My fridge broke down, the toaster died,
The microwave just sat and cried,
The toilet lost its urge to flush,
The freezer contents turned to mush!

'The vacuum cleaner doesn't suck,
The coffee maker runs amuck,
The oven smokes, the dryer too,
The washer coughs as though on cue.'

—'Murphy's Law!', Terry Fitterer

The lines of this poem illustrate the adage known as Murphy's law, which states that 'Anything that can go wrong will go wrong'. I particularly like the line 'The vacuum cleaner doesn't suck'. While this literally means the appliance doesn't do its job of sucking up dirt, there's a little joke packed into it: in American slang, when you say 'something sucks', it means that something is bad or frustrating. So, saying the vacuum cleaner 'doesn't suck' can also mean that it works well—creating a witty contradiction.

I used to think that Murphy's law was just an interesting name made up for the adage. I was surprised to discover that the Murphy in Murphy's law was a real person. His full name was Edward Murphy. He was an American aerospace engineer who worked on a project at the Edwards Air Force Base in California in the 1940s.

But Murphy doesn't get all the credit for coming up with Murphy's law. At least a part of the credit goes to Dr John Stapp, a US Air Force colonel. From 1948 to 1949, Stapp headed the research project at the air force base to test the human tolerance for g-forces during rapid deceleration. The tests were performed using a rocket sled mounted on a railroad track. Stapp was his own guinea pig. He would strap himself to the sled and try to measure the g-forces on himself when applying the brakes once the rocket sled was going super-fast. But he wasn't able to get an accurate measurement.

Murphy suggested a certain type of gauge to measure the g-forces correctly. Curiously, this time, they decided to use a chimpanzee instead of Dr Stapp as the guinea pig. Imagine a chimpanzee barrelling down a railroad track on a rocket sled. It must have been frightened half to death! Unfortunately, Murphy's assistant installed the gauges incorrectly, so the experiment failed. That's when an annoyed Murphy said, 'If there's any way to do it wrong, he will find it.'

Later, after the problems were sorted out, a press conference was held. There, Stapp was asked how there were no major injuries during the tests. This is when he recast Murphy's statement and presented it as Murphy's law: 'Anything that can go wrong, will go wrong.' Stapp announced that it was because they took Murphy's law into account that they could avoid accidents. They used the law to consider all possible things that could go wrong and then pre-empted them.

So the original use of Murphy's law was in a positive sense—as an approach to avoid accidents and failures through foresight. Murphy's law was a catchy idea with a catchy name and it quickly caught on. It appealed to the public at large, not because it helped them pre-empt problems, but as a darkly humorous way to describe everything going wrong. Soon, people started coming up with their own interesting variations on the statement.

American author Arthur Bloch wrote a series of books on Murphy's law and its many variations. His first book is titled *Murphy's Law and Other Reasons Why Things Go Wrong!* In some versions of the book, the word 'wrong' in the title is printed upside down or shown with a letter falling out of it as a humorous nod to the law.

An optimistic take on Murphy's law is Yhprum's law, which states, 'Anything that can go right, will go right.' In case you haven't guessed it, Yhprum is Murphy spelt backwards.

Yet another variation—and deliberate misspelling—is called Muphry's law. And this law is one that I need to be mindful of, because it's relevant to English nuts. It says, 'If you write anything criticizing editing or proofreading, there will be a fault of some kind in what you have written.'

The American Dialect Society is a society dedicated to the study of the English language. Its members have researched Murphy's law to see if the idea really originated with Murphy and Stapp. What they have found is that similar statements had been made long before Stapp and Murphy came up with it. For example, in 1866, British mathematician Augustus De Morgan wrote: 'The first experiment already illustrates a truth of the theory, well confirmed by practice, what-ever can happen will happen if we make enough trials.' De Morgan, who's famous for De Morgan's laws, was born in Madurai, India, in 1806.

Of course, his statement is not quite the same as the version associated with Edward Murphy. We don't really know whether statements like this provided inspiration for Murphy's law as we know it today.

Here's one last witty corollary to the law: it's called Mrs Murphy's law. It says, 'Anything that can go wrong will go wrong while Mr Murphy is out of town.'

A couple of example sentences from my own life:

> 'I brought an umbrella every day this week except today, and of course it poured. Classic Murphy's law.'
> 'I wore my brand-new white shirt for the first time, and Murphy's law ensured I spilled curry on it.'

Now tell me, have you ever experienced Murphy's law?

48

A dish fit for the gods

'On their first date, Angad cooked a dish fit for the gods. For Meghna, it was love at first bite.' That was an example of how we might use the idiom 'a dish fit for the gods' to talk about superlative food.

But this idiom originally had a lot more bite to it. In fact, it was quite murderous. If we recall the way Shakespeare first used it in his play *Julius Caesar* (1599), we may never again want to apply it to the food we eat.

The play tells the story of Julius Caesar's friend Brutus and others who decide to assassinate Caesar as they are unhappy with his growing power.

The following are Brutus' words to Caius, his co-conspirator, as they plan the murder:

> Our course will seem too bloody, Caius Cassius,
> To cut the head off and then hack the limbs,
> Like wrath in death and envy afterwards,
> [...]
> Let's kill him boldly, but not wrathfully;
> Let's carve him as a dish fit for the gods,
> Not hew him as a carcass fit for hounds.
>
> (*Julius Caesar*, Act 2, Scene 1)

Brutus was mindful that they should not tear Caesar from limb to limb—an act that would make them look like butchers.

A dish fit for the gods

He knew it would be better to position himself and his co-conspirators as noble citizens who reluctantly sacrificed Caesar to save the Roman Republic, which was being endangered by the concentration of power in Caesar's hands. That is why the plan was to kill Caesar in such a way that his corpse would be seen as a sacrificial offering fit for the gods.

Caesar might have saved himself from being assassinated had he paid heed to the portents that came his way. His wife had had an ominous dream and she had begged Caesar not to go to the meeting of the Senate. He had also been told by a stranger, an unknown soothsayer, to 'Beware the Ides of March'. But despite this warning and his wife's dream, Caesar allowed himself to be lured to the meeting hall at the Curia of Pompey where he was murdered.

When I first read the statement 'Beware the Ides of March' I was mystified by it. What did it mean?

It turns out that the date 15 March was called the Ides of March. In fact, according to the Roman calendar, the middle day of every month was called ides. Or rather, *idus*, the word in Latin from which 'ides' is derived. The Ides of March, of course, became notorious in the annals of Roman history as the day in the year 44 BCE when Caesar was assassinated.

'A woman is a dish for the gods'—this line, which is similar to the one we have been discussing, appears in Shakespeare's *Antony and Cleopatra* (1623), Act 5, Scene 2.

In the climax of this play, when Cleopatra is about to take her own life, a clown appears. Clowns and jesters often appear in Shakespeare's plays to convey significant facts or ideas. Cleopatra asks him if the snake that has been brought to her as the instrument of her suicide would eat her. The clown replies: 'A woman is a dish for the gods, if the devil dress her not.' In other words, women are made for the gods, except those corrupted by evil.

Bloodshed. Murder. Suicide. These are the origins of 'dish fit for the gods'. I love the salad known as Caesar salad and used to think of it as a dish fit for the gods. But after knowing what that idiom originally meant, I am not so sure.

49

If they have no bread, let them eat cake

These are the most famous words that Marie Antoinette, the queen of France, never said. And yet, the words were partly responsible for her death.

The quote represents the indifference of the royalty to the poverty of the masses—which was one of the reasons that the French Revolution happened in 1789. The upshot of the revolution was that the rulers of France, King Louis XVI and his wife Marie Antoinette, were stripped of their powers, imprisoned and then executed. France became a republic ruled by a democratically elected government rather than the *ancien régime,* the centuries-old system of hereditary monarchy and feudalism. Of course, things weren't so black and white. The fledgling democracy went through many ups and downs in the years after the revolution.

'If they have no bread, let them eat cake!' is a translation of the French quote, '*S'ils n'ont plus de pain, qu'ils mangent de la brioche!*'

The literal translation of this sentence is 'If they don't have any more bread, let them eat brioche'. Brioche is not cake but because it's a rich, sweet bread, it conveys the same point: an apparent lack of understanding of—and apathy towards—the fact that if the poor cannot afford something as basic as bread, they certainly cannot afford a far more expensive (and indulgent) food item.

However, the story about the bread and brioche was most likely just that—a story. It was probably inspired by the *Confessions* of philosopher Jean-Jacques Rousseau. Book VI of Rousseau's *Confessions* mentions an unnamed 'great princess' making a similar statement. This princess could not have been Marie Antoinette as she was a mere child in 1767, the year in or around which the book was written. Moreover, she was an Austrian princess, and came to Versailles—the seat of the French royal family—only in 1770. And she became queen even later, in 1774.

Rousseau may have been inspired by similar stories that existed in folklore in different parts of Europe. The theme of such stories was the insensitivity of the nobility or royalty towards peasants, due to a lack of understanding of the harsh reality of their lives. In a tale from sixteenth-century Germany, for example, a noblewoman asks why the starving poor do not eat a sweet bread called *krosem*.

The anecdote that spread throughout France on the eve of the French Revolution was that, while riding around in her coach, the queen had asked why the peasants looked unhappy. She was told by her page that it was because they had no bread, their staple food. This was the year 1789. The harvest had failed, the people were starving, and the price of bread was sky-high. Against this backdrop, Marie Antoinette supposedly stated, 'If they have no bread, let them eat cake!'

Apart from the famine conditions due to crop failure, the economy was drained by the country's financial support of the American War of Independence against the British. While these were the real causes of the dire conditions, the masses blamed the extravagant lifestyle of the queen. Due to her spendthrift nature, they even gave her the nickname Madame Déficit. Even at a time of acute financial crisis and food shortage, she indulged in excesses, such as the fortune she spent on building herself a private retreat called the Hameau de la Reine or the Queen's Hamlet.

The people of France had come to hate the queen and were ready to believe that she had indeed made the statement. The hatred was fuelled not just by rumours but by plays and pamphlets that portrayed her as an extravagant, eccentric and immoral woman.

And thus began the rapid downfall of the queen.

In 1789, the bleak financial and political situation forced King Louis XVI to summon the Estates General. These were the representatives of the three estates in French society: the First Estate was the Catholic clergy, the Second Estate was the nobility, and the Third Estate comprised everyone else—from peasant farmers to the relatively wealthy people called the bourgeoisie.

At the meeting of the Estates General, the finance minister spoke about the budget deficit and claimed that the new taxes would make up for it. But the commoners were dissatisfied with this solution and decided to take matters into their own hands. And thus the French Revolution began.

The king and queen were deposed, imprisoned and put on trial a few years later—first the king and then the queen. Louis XVI was beheaded on 21 January 1793.

Marie Antoinette's trial by the Revolutionary Tribunal began on 14 October 1793. The tribunal sped up the legal proceedings and sentenced her to death. They declared the queen the 'scourge and the blood-sucker of the French'.

They took the queen to the guillotine in an open cart with her hair chopped off. She had been famed for her elaborate hairstyles, so this was yet another form of humiliation.

On 16 October 1793, Marie Antoinette was guillotined at

the Place de la Révolution in Paris—a place now known as Place de la Concorde.

People have largely forgotten the dignity with which Marie Antoinette spoke at her trial and her composure at the guillotine. The one thing she is remembered for is something she never said.

And yet, it cost her her head.

50

One fell swoop

I've been using the phrase 'in/at one fell swoop' for years. I knew it referred to things happening or being done all at once, in a single swift action. I used the idiom in sentences such as the following ones:

> 'His hopes of becoming a Bollywood star were dashed in one fell swoop.'
> 'At the peak of the Covid-19 pandemic, she lost her husband, her home and her job at one fell swoop.'
> 'The tsunami destroyed the island city in one fell swoop.'
> 'The social media companies took away our privacy at one fell swoop.'

Despite my frequent usage of the phrase, I hadn't given much thought to the meaning of the word 'fell' in it. It was obviously not being used as the past tense of 'fall'.

Well, it turns out that it is an old adjective that, according to the *Oxford English Dictionary*, meant 'fierce, cruel, ruthless; terrible, destructive'. 'Fell' in this sense survives mainly in this idiom. The earliest usage of the word dates back to the late thirteenth century. It is related to the Old French *fel*, which comes from the Middle Latin *fello*, meaning 'villain' or 'traitor'. It is linked to the word 'felon', which used to mean 'a wicked person'.

Somewhere down the line I realized that this idiom came from Shakespeare's *Macbeth*. Like many other phrases, this one was either invented or popularized by Shakespeare. His play certainly contains the first documented use of it.

Macbeth, a Scottish general, discovers three witches on a bleak Scottish moor. The witches prophesy that he will be the future king of Scotland. His ambition thus whetted and then egged on by his wife, Lady Macbeth, he assassinates Duncan, the reigning king, and ascends the throne.

However, he is racked by paranoia and ends up killing anyone he perceives as a threat. But the murder of the family of Macduff—a legendary Scottish hero who is the antagonist to Macbeth's protagonist—marks the moment when Macbeth descends into utter madness, because he has nothing to gain from this killing. He does however have a lot to lose from it, as it turns out, because Macbeth eventually dies at the hand of Macduff.

When Macduff discovers that his wife and children have been murdered by Macbeth's agents, he cries out:

> All my pretty ones?
> Did you say all? O hell-kite! All?
> What, all my pretty chickens and their dam
> At one fell swoop?

> (*Macbeth*, Act 4 Scene 3)

The dictionary definition of 'swoop' is the sudden, swift dive of birds to attack somebody or something. In this context, they are usually birds of prey, such as eagles and vultures, which make a swift dive, or swoop, to kill animals for food.

Here, poor Macduff likens the killer of his family to the kite, a hunting bird, swooping down from hell and killing his helpless chickens, his children, and their mother, the dam (the female parent of an animal).

One fell swoop

Over time, the meaning of 'one fell swoop' has lost its original savagery. It is no longer about a violent act necessarily, but merely a sudden one where things are done at one go:

> 'The guests were so hungry the snacks disappeared in one fell swoop.'
> 'He completed his Diwali shopping at one fell swoop.'
> 'The new law criminalized all forms of discrimination at one fell swoop.'

The acts described in these sentences are benign—unlike the ones in the first lot of examples I gave you. Each of those had the sense of a terrible blow.

You may hear people say 'one foul swoop', where foul is spelt with a 'u', or 'one fowl swoop', where it's spelt with a 'w'. These are mistakes—people getting muddled by the unfamiliar word 'fell'. But 'one swell foop' is not a mistake. It's a deliberate distortion used in a jocular way. It is a useful joke—with 'swell' serving as a reminder that 'fell', which rhymes with it, is the correct word to use.

51
Dead ringer / Saved by the bell / Graveyard shift

dead ringer

If I tell you that you're a dead ringer for Ranveer Singh, it means you look exactly like the film star. Or you could be a dead ringer for Alia Bhatt—meaning you look exactly like her. 'Dead ringer' means 'an exact duplicate', unlike the so-called duplicates in Bollywood who can pass for the originals only from a distance or in the dark.

There is a fascinating theory that the phrase dead ringer originated in the graveyard. The story is that back in the day, people who were unconscious but not quite dead would sometimes be mistakenly buried alive! In some cases, when the bodies were later exhumed, scratch marks were found inside the coffin—presumably because the buried person woke up and tried to claw their way out of the grave. It's suffocating just to think about it, isn't it?

Well, apparently, this led to the practice of tying one end of a long string to the finger of the deceased through a hole in the coffin. The other end of the string was tied to the church bell. If the body came to life, the movement of the hand would make the church bell ring. This person who rang the church bell—usually in the middle of the night—was called a dead ringer!

It's a deliciously creepy story. One that might keep you

awake at night. But I'm sorry to disappoint you if you believed it. As stories of this nature go, it is not rooted in fact and cannot be substantiated.

The term dead ringer actually comes from horse racing. It originated in the practice of substituting an identical-looking slow horse with a fast one for a crooked advantage in betting.

An article in the *Manitoba Free Press* from 1882 first defined 'ringer': 'A horse that is taken through the country and trotted under a false name and pedigree is called a "ringer."'

The first confirmed use of *dead* ringer to mean an exact duplicate came a few years later in the *Oshkosh Weekly Times*. A June 1888 issue contains a court report of a man charged with being 'very drunk': '"Dat ar is a markable semlance be shoo", said Hart looking critically at the picture. "Dat's a dead ringer fo me. I nebber done see such a semblence."'

Please do not use the spellings from this quote. 'Dat' is meant to be 'that'. 'Fo' is actually 'for'. And 'semlance' and 'semblence' are both corruptions of 'semblance', used here to mean 'resemblance'. You can probably guess the correct forms of the other drunken distortions.

'Ringer' is a term that has been used in various contexts to refer to an identical copy—particularly when the copy is an illegal one. Car ringing, for example, means replacing the identification numbers of a stolen car with legitimate ones from another vehicle, one which may have been scrapped.

The word 'dead' is not used in the sense of lifeless in 'dead ringer'. It means 'exact'. If that surprises you, think of the term 'dead centre'. It means the exact centre, right?

saved by the bell

Let's revisit the dead body that came back to life in the coffin. It moved its hands about and the string tied to one of its fingers made the church bell ring. Alerted by the sound, the person keeping watch swiftly dug up the coffin and saved the buried person from suffocating to death. The phrase 'saved by the bell' would apply nicely to this situation, right? And there is a theory that this is the origin of that particular phrase. Quite interesting, isn't it?

But alas, once again, fact is less interesting than fiction.

Before getting to the actual origin of the phrase, let's understand its meaning and usage. 'Saved by the bell' means narrowly escaping having to do or say something you don't want to. Or being spared from a difficulty or misfortune by a last-minute occurrence.

'Saved by the bell' is an allusion to a knocked-down boxer who is saved from being counted 'out' thanks to the bell announcing the end of the round. Normally, if a boxer is knocked down, he must get up unaided before the referee finishes counting to ten. Otherwise, he is deemed knocked out from the fight. However, if the bell signalling the end of the round rings before the referee's count ends, it buys the boxer a little more time to get up and move to the next round of the fight.

'Saved by the bell' became a part of boxing slang in the second half of the nineteenth century. One of the earliest documented references to it is from an 1893 issue of the *Fitchburg Sentinel* of Massachusetts, USA: 'Martin Flaherty defeated Bobby Burns in 32 rounds by a complete knockout. Half a dozen times, Flaherty was saved by the bell in the earlier rounds.'

Even if you're not a boxer, you can use the phrase to describe tight situations you narrowly got out of:

> 'My father was about to catch me watching a movie instead of studying, but my mother called out to him and he turned away from my door. Saved by the bell!'

> 'I did not know the answer to the teacher's question, but the period came to an end right before she could ask me to speak. I was literally saved by the bell!'
>
> 'The electricity went just as my mother asked me to iron my shirt—a chore I despise. I was saved by the bell.'

These examples are a far cry from a person buried alive ringing church bells. A far cry from boxing, too.

graveyard shift

The last of this trio of phrases is 'the graveyard shift'. There is a social media forward that attributes its origin to the night shift at the graveyard when someone would have to keep watch in case the 'dead ringer' rang the church bell. The person assigned this shift could help pull the person buried alive out of the grave, and so the latter would literally be saved by the bell. But, of course, this origin story is yet another fabricated one.

The graveyard shift is a term coined in the US for a late-night or early-morning shift at work. It too was invented in the late nineteenth century. It probably got its name from the eerie atmosphere of a deserted workplace manned by a skeleton staff at night and does not have anything to do with an actual graveyard. And before your imagination runs away with you, 'skeleton staff' just means minimal staff.

You may use 'graveyard shift' in sentences like these:

> 'He didn't mind the graveyard shift; the quiet hours gave him time to write.'
>
> 'The nurse braced herself for another long night of the graveyard shift at the hospital.'

An 1897 issue of *The Salt Lake Tribune* contains this quote: 'The police changed shifts for the month yesterday. This month

Sergeant Ware takes the morning relief. Sergeant Matt Rhodes the middle and Sergeant John Burbidge the graveyard shift.'

And that completes the trio of phrases with fake origin stories.

52

Hair of the dog / Let the cat out of the bag

hair of the dog

Say you've been bitten by a rabid dog on the street. You're infected with rabies, a deadly disease. So you go back to the afflicted dog to get a hair from it—probably getting bitten again in the process. Then you apply that hair to your wounds. In the olden days this procedure was believed to be a cure for dog bites and rabies.

Of course, medicine has advanced since then, and it's common knowledge now that someone bitten by a rabid dog should immediately get an anti-rabies shot administered.

The present-day usage of 'hair of the dog' does not refer to dogs or rabies though. It has more to do with the hangover you get from drinking too much alcohol. When you take a small drink the morning after a night of heavy drinking, it is called the hair of the dog. It may give you some temporary relief from the symptoms of alcohol poisoning that you're experiencing.

Interestingly, the earliest documented use of the phrase according to the *Oxford English Dictionary* is in this figurative sense. It is found in the 1546 text *A Dialogue Conteinyng the Number in Effect of All the Prouerbes in the Englishe Tongue* by English writer John Heywood:

I pray thee let me and my fellow have
A hair of the dog that bit us last night—
And bitten were we both to the brain aright.
We saw each other drunk in the good ale glass.

The reference here is clearly to alcohol and not dog bites.

The first reference to the literal use of the hair of the dog to cure bite wounds seems to appear more than two centuries later in 1760. English physician Robert James writes about it in *A Treatise on Canine Madness*: 'The hair of the dog that gave the wound is advised as an application to the part injured.' But even that long ago, a time when there were strange beliefs about medical treatments, James was sceptical about this particular cure.

'Hair of the dog' is an unusual case where we find examples of its figurative use—in the sense of a hangover remedy—much before we come across its literal use.

One more century on, in 1898, we find both the literal and figurative use explained in the *Dictionary of Phrase and Fable* by the clergyman, school teacher and lexicographer Ebenezer Cobham Brewer:

> In Scotland it is a popular belief that a few hairs of the dog that bit you applied to the wound will prevent evil consequences. Applied to drinks, it means, if overnight you have indulged too freely, take a glass of the same wine within 24 hours to soothe the nerves. *If this dog do you bite, soon as out of your bed, take a hair of the tail the next day.*

Here's how we can use the phrase in a sentence:

> 'Ritesh wasn't sure if the whiskey helped or hurt, but the hair of the dog was a ritual he swore by.'
> 'Rita groaned, clutching her head, and muttered, "Only the hair of the dog can save me now."'

let the cat out of the bag

To 'let the cat out of the bag' is to disclose a secret either deliberately or inadvertently. If you've ever blurted out a surprise party plan to the guest of honour, congratulations—you've let the cat out of the bag. But why a cat? And why a bag? The origin of the idiom is not clear.

There are two theories. One, which dates back to the Middle Ages, is about a scam which involves selling a cat in the name of a piglet. It's related to the phrase 'a pig in a poke'. A 'poke' is an old-fashioned term for a bag. The idiom refers to something, a suckling pig for example, that is bought without being properly seen or inspected. So if a shady livestock seller put a cat in a bag instead of a piglet, the scam would be revealed only when the buyer went home and 'let the cat out of the bag'. The only problem with this theory is that a cat is much lighter than a pig. Even a small pig.

The second theory has to do with a similar saying in Spanish: *dar gato por liebre*, which means 'to give a cat instead of a hare'. It's used in the context of being scammed by a vendor who has passed off something cheap in place of something more valuable. Note that the 'hair' in the 'hair of the dog' is spelt 'h-a-i-r'. But in this Spanish phrase we're talking about a hare—spelt 'h-a-r-e'—meaning the mammal that resembles a rabbit.

This idiom has an interesting history. It came out of sixteenth- and seventeenth-century Spain, when people used to go on long journeys on foot or horseback. Travelling by day, they would stay the night at *posada*s or inns. The innkeepers would sometimes serve these travellers cat meat in place of hare because the latter was much more expensive.

In fact, this scam was so common that travellers would utter an incantation before their meal:

Si eres cabrito, mantente frito;
Si eres gato, salta al plato.

(If you're goat meat, stay fried;
If you're cat meat, jump on the plate.)

Given that a cat has nine lives, perhaps it could actually come alive—even after being cooked—and give the wily innkeeper away!

The other theory about letting the cat out of the bag is linked to the nine-tailed whip called cat o' nine tails, which was used in the British Royal Navy to flog errant sailors. Apparently the whip was stored in a red sack and so a sailor who revealed the wrongdoings of another would be letting the cat out of the bag—'cat' being short for cat o' nine tails. As in, the cat or whip would be removed from the bag to whip the sailor with. But, just as in the case of the marketplace scam, this story is not backed by proof.

The oldest reference to the phrase in print is from a 1760 book review in *The London Magazine*. The reviewer 'wished that the author had not let the cat out of the bag', a sort of old-style request for a 'spoiler alert'.

It's an interesting coincidence that 1760 is the year that marks both the first use of 'letting the cat out of the bag' and the literal use of 'hair of the dog'.

This first record of the feline-related phrase, however, gives us no clue about its actual origin. My own, totally unfounded, theory is that English people who knew little Spanish heard the phrase 'dar gato por liebre' and mistook the word *liebre*, which means 'hare', to be *libre*, which means 'free', and mistranslated the phrase to mean 'freeing the cat that was in the bag'—which is how the English saying came into being. But let me stress that this is a totally unfounded theory. I threw it in just for fun. Don't take it seriously.

Here are some ways to use this phrase:

> 'Manasi didn't look surprised at her "surprise" birthday party. The caterer had let the cat out of the bag when he called for directions.'
>
> 'Sujoy was beaming. The HR head had let the cat out of the bag about his upcoming promotion.'
>
> 'Abhishek confided in me about his affair. But I let the cat out of the bag, as I am generally prone to, being a gossip columnist for a film magazine. He's now furious with me.'

53
Hot-blooded

'Well, I'm hot blooded, check it and see
I got a fever of a hundred and three
Come on baby, do you do more than dance?
I'm hot blooded, I'm hot blooded'

—'Hot Blooded', Foreigner

I used to sing along with this number as a hot-blooded youth. It was a hugely popular song that, aptly, reached the #3 position on the *Billboard* Hot 100 chart.

'Hot-blooded' means 'passionate, aroused or angry'. And, of course, it was coined by that hot-blooded playwright, William Shakespeare. The expression made its first appearance in his comedy *The Merry Wives of Windsor*.

Falstaff, a naughty knight, decides to woo two ladies at the same time. What makes his plan naughtier still is that both these ladies are married. The ladies—the Merry Wives—are on to him, but they decide to play along to have some fun at his expense and teach him a lesson into the bargain.

As instructed by the Merry Wives, Falstaff comes to meet them in Windsor Forest disguised as Herne the Hunter—a phantom with antlers on his head who was said to haunt the royal forest near Windsor Castle. As Falstaff arrives with lustful anticipation, he soliloquizes:

> The Windsor bell hath struck twelve;
> the minute draws on. Now, the hot-blooded
> gods assist me!
>
> (Act 5, Scene 5)

But Falstaff's desires are thwarted as, in accordance with the Merry Wives' plans, children dressed as fairies attack him the moment he gets there.

When Falstaff realizes that the joke's on him, he accepts the situation sportingly, thus partially redeeming himself.

One little piece of trivia before we leave Windsor Forest: *The Merry Wives of Windsor* is the only Shakespeare comedy that's set in England! Surprising, isn't it?

Shakespeare uses the adjective 'hot-blooded' again a few years later in the tragedy *King Lear*. The old king decides to divide his kingdom among his three daughters based on their avowals of love for him. He ends up splitting his kingdom between his two older daughters, Goneril and Regan, who go over the top with their declarations of affection. He disinherits the youngest, Cordelia, in anger when she says she loves her father as per the bond between them—no more, no less. Her crime? She does not wish to profit from an exaggerated show of love like her sisters.

By the time Lear realizes the truth about the two older daughters, it is too late. He has given up his power to them and they now mistreat him. Meanwhile, despite the fact that Cordelia loses her dowry—her share of the kingdom—one of her suitors, the king of France, is impressed by her honesty and wants to marry her. He takes her back to France with him. King Lear sees this as an act of impetuosity or passion on his part—a sign of his 'hot-blooded' nature.

All King Lear wants in his old age is to live with dignity

with either one of the two elder daughters. But they play a humiliating game of ping pong with him. When Regan asks King Lear to go live with Goneril despite her ill treatment of him, he says:

> [...] Return with her?
> Why the hot-blooded France, that dowerless took
> Our youngest borne, I could as well be brought
> To knee his Throne, and Squire-like pension beg,
> To keep base life a foot; return with her?
>
> (Act 2, Scene 4)

Here's a quote from more recent literature: In his 2011 book *Dead Rules*, author Randy Russell writes, 'Mars knew that love wasn't all red-paper valentines and candy hearts. Love wasn't always joy. Love could be hot-blooded pain down to the bone. Sometimes love was despair. And sometimes love was wrong.'

I'll let the English model and TV personality Tamara Ecclestone have the last word: 'My mum is Croatian, and obviously she's female and she's very emotional, very hot-blooded, very touchy-feely, whereas I think my dad's quite British.'

I wonder what she means when she says her father is 'quite British'!

54

Red herring

A red herring, in the literal sense, is a dried, smoked herring. What's a herring, you ask? Well, it's a long silver-coloured fish. Large schools of these fish swim in the sea. Their flesh is white when fresh. The process of smoking (a preservation and flavouring method) turns them red.

At one point in my school years, reading a book was synonymous with devouring an Agatha Christie murder mystery. Those books were my introduction to the 'red herring' in the figurative sense.

In *Murder on the Orient Express*, perhaps Christie's finest detective novel, her legendary Belgian sleuth Hercule Poirot travels to London on the Orient Express. A murder takes place on the train in the wee hours. How Poirot gets the first intimation of something fishy going on is described in this passage from the book:

> He was just dropping off when something again woke him.
> This time it was as though something heavy had fallen with a thud against the door.
> He sprang up, opened it and looked out. Nothing. But to his right, some distance down the corridor, a woman wrapped in a scarlet kimono was retreating from him. [...]
> Everything was deathly quiet.

In the investigations that follow, Poirot asks each of the ladies on board if she has a scarlet kimono. They all deny it. Later, the kimono mysteriously lands up in Poirot's suitcase. This dress seems to be the key to the murder but ultimately turns out to be a red herring—a distraction, a plot device deliberately designed to throw the reader off the trail of the real murderer.

In this sense, the red herring is a literary device that leads readers towards a false conclusion.

In *The Da Vinci Code* by Dan Brown, Bishop Aringarosa is made to appear as the villain of the piece but this later turns out to not be the case. Interestingly, the Italian words *aringa rosa* translate to 'pink herring' in English. And if you add an 's' in the bishop's name, it becomes *aringa rossa*, which literally translates to 'red herring'. And, of course, the character Aringarosa is a classic red herring in the novel.

A Study in Scarlet, written in 1887 by Sir Arthur Conan Doyle, is the detective novel that introduced the world to Sherlock Holmes and his associate Dr Watson. In this story, the word *rache*, German for 'revenge', is found written at the scene of the murder. This is a red herring that misleads you into thinking that a German was responsible for the crime.

The figurative use of 'red herring' has its roots in an 1807 article written by journalist William Cobbett, lambasting the British press for erroneously reporting the defeat of Napoleon. Cobbett mentions that he had once used a red herring to distract hounds that were pursuing a hare. And he uses 'red-herring' figuratively in the following statement: 'It was a mere transitory effect of the political red-herring; for, on the Saturday, the scent became as cold as a stone.' The *Oxford English Dictionary* says that this use of 'red herring' by Cobbett and his extensive repetition of it in 1833 established the phrase. It also established something else—the mistaken notion that red herrings were used by huntsmen to train hounds to not be distracted from a trail.

Red herring

The story goes that red herrings were used to train hounds to follow the scent of the prey—a fox or badger, perhaps. The very smelly red herring was dragged at 90 degrees to the trail that the dogs were meant to follow in order to confuse them. Eventually the dogs would learn to follow the fainter scent of the prey without being distracted by the red herring—a parallel, in a way, to the figurative use of red herring as we know it today.

Brewer's Dictionary of Phrase and Fable (1981) records the idiom as 'drawing a red herring across the path'. The definition given: 'to divert attention from the main question by some side issue'. However, the theory that there was an actual practice of confusing dogs to help train them turned out to be incorrect. There is some evidence, though, that red herrings were used to *guide horses* along a trail rather than *distract hounds* from one.

Another version of the origin story is that in the 1800s, British fugitives used the strong-smelling red herring to throw hounds off their trail.

Next, the research trail leads us to something called a red herring prospectus. This is a preliminary document issued to potential investors by a company as a part of a public offering of stocks or bonds. It does not have complete information about the price and number of shares being issued and hence can be misleading. So American bankers in the 1920s dubbed it a red herring prospectus—to warn investors about its potential pitfalls.

Going beyond literary devices and unreliable documents to everyday life, a red herring is something that misleads or distracts from a relevant or important question.

Politicians often use red herrings. You ask them something that they don't have a satisfactory answer for, and they change the topic. If questioned about rising prices, for example, they may ask you to think about our soldiers fighting at the border. That's a red herring.

You and I use red herrings in everyday conversation without even realizing it. A colleague tells you, 'My boss rejected my ideas. Now I have to work all night to meet the deadline.' You respond, 'You think you're having a bad day? The trains aren't running today. I had to walk two hours to get to work.' You just used a red herring.

If a child passing a toy store says, 'Mummy, I want that train set. It looks like so much fun!' Mummy might answer, 'But you have those fun toy cars at home, let's go and play with them.' Mummy just distracted the kid with a red herring.

These are examples of what's known as a red herring fallacy, to use a slightly more technical term. In such an argument, the red herring diverts you from the main point by focusing on a detail and building that into a new argument.

55

Ears are burning

Are you talking about me? Because my ears are burning.

Wait, one of my ears has stopped burning. The right one. Now only my left ear is burning. That's not good. It means somebody's saying something bad about me behind my back.

If someone were saying something nice, my right ear would be burning.

At least, that's what the Romans believed—that a tingling or burning sensation in your hearing apparatus meant you were being talked about. And if only one ear were burning, you could determine whether they were saying good things or bad.

These beliefs are linked to the tradition of augury in ancient Rome. Augurs were priests whose duty it was to 'read' natural phenomena ranging from the flight pattern of birds to the entrails of animals to predict upcoming events or interpret the will of the gods. Their purview extended to bodily sensations and the rule of thumb was that things connected to the left side spelt evil. Speaking of thumbs, a pricking sensation in the left thumb was said to portend evil. A flickering right eye, on the other hand, was interpreted to mean that a friend was going to visit.

In 77 CE, the Roman scholar Pliny wrote in his 37-volume encyclopaedia *Naturalis Historia*, 'Those absent are warned by a ringing of the ears when they are being talked about.' (Volume 28, Chapter 5) Such beliefs are reflected in the works of Roman playwright Plautus as well.

While we no longer have priests called augurs today, the word 'augur' is still used to talk about a happening or thing indicating a good or bad outcome:

> 'The salary he was offered did not augur well for his status in the new company he joined.'
> 'The first quarter figures augur well for the company's performance this financial year.'

The phrase was first used in Chaucer's poem, *Troilus and Criseyde*, written in the 1380s: 'And when thou art gone, I trust, we shall speak of thee somewhat to make thine ears glow'. Chaucer's poem was written in Middle English, which is difficult to follow, so I just quoted the modern English 'translation' of it. Of course, the word used by him is 'glow' and not 'burn' making it more elegant. You could choose to use this version of the phrase too if you wish to sound more refined. But you may have to explain to the listener what you mean!

The first appearance of the expression with the word 'burn' in it specifically is in a sixteenth-century poem by James Yates. The poem is found in a collection called *The Castell of Courtesie*, published in 1582. It goes:

> That I doe credite give unto the saying old:
> Which is, when as the eares doe burne, some thing on
>   thee is told

Is there any truth to this belief about tingling ears? Is it possible that you become subconsciously aware that others are talking about you and that awareness manifests itself in a sensation in your ears? Perhaps, perhaps!

Sometimes, you can use the phrase when you actually overhear people talking about you. Shakespeare employs a version of the phrase in this way in his play *Much Ado About*

Nothing. The character Beatrice overhears two others, Hero and Ursula, talking about her. This is her reaction:

> What fire is in mine ears? Can this be true?
> Stand I condemned for pride and scorn so much?
>
> (Act 3, Scene 1)

The idea of a fire in the ears is how Shakespeare poetically expresses the idea of ears burning.

Now, it could be that you are the one who has been talking about someone else in his or her absence. In that case, you may say to the person when you meet him or her, 'Were your ears burning? We were just talking about you. All good things, of course.'

56

Wear your heart on your sleeve / Foam at the mouth

wear your heart on your sleeve

> I wear my heart on my sleeve,
> Don't count the cost,
> If I can't live in love then surely I've lost.
>
> ('Heart on My Sleeve', Gallagher & Lyle,
> covered by Ringo Starr)

These words sung by Ringo Starr resonate with me.

They are from the song titled 'Heart on My Sleeve'. Ringo Starr, who shot to fame as the drummer of the celebrated British musical band The Beatles, sang this song as a solo artist after the quartet split up. According to the song, life is all about love—you should unabashedly wear your heart on your sleeve without worrying about the negative consequences of being vulnerable.

'Wearing your heart on your sleeve' means to openly show your feelings—romantic or otherwise.

Actually, I think whether you do so or not depends on your personality. For example, it's in my nature to wear my heart on my sleeve. Life has tried to teach me to be guarded about my feelings, but I am still not good at it.

This idiom about hearts and sleeves may have originated in

Heart on your sleeve / Foam at the mouth

jousting. Jousting is a sporting contest that knights participated in during the Middle Ages. It involved fighting with lances on horseback. A knight wore a scarf or ribbon of the lady he loved on his arm during the match. As usual, this theory is not proven. Though, as is also usual, the first recorded use of the idiom is by Shakespeare. It's in his 1604 play, *Othello*. The dastardly character Iago pretends to wear his heart on his sleeve to appear faithful to Othello:

> But I will wear my heart upon my sleeve
> For daws to peck at: I am not what I am.
>
> (Act 1, Scene 1)

Here are a few ways you can use the phrase:

> 'In certain societies, it's considered inappropriate for a man to wear his heart on his sleeve—so he's encouraged to bottle up his feelings.'
> 'What attracted Shaina to Shekhar was the fact that he wore his heart on his sleeve.'
> 'When fighting corporate politics, one shouldn't wear one's heart on one's sleeve.'

foam at the mouth

To 'foam at the mouth' literally means 'to spew saliva with little air bubbles in it'. Figuratively, it means 'to appear extremely angry'—to be visibly enraged, furious. Some believe that the expression comes from people or animals afflicted with rabies. This disease causes sufferers to behave aggressively and to foam at the mouth.

Shakespeare used the phrase in his play *Julius Caesar* (Act 1, Scene 2) in 1601: 'He fell down in the market-place, and foamed at mouth, and was speechless.'

This is the first known use of the phrase. It refers to Caesar having some sort of seizure after getting worked up about refusing the crown he was being offered.

Shakespeare used it a second time in the play *Cymbeline* (Act 5, Scene 5), written c. 1610:

> [...] Lord Cloten,
> Upon my lady's missing, came to me
> With his sword drawn;
> foam'd at the mouth, and swore,
> If I discover'd not which way she was gone,
> It was my instant death.

Here's an example of more recent vintage. In 2015, journalist Amrit Dhillon wrote in *The National* about the alleged obscenity of a TV show: 'That didn't stop outraged television anchors foaming at the mouth about how "the modesty of Indian culture" had been desecrated.'

Here's how you can use the idiom in regular everyday sentences:

> 'I foam at the mouth whenever I hear my arch nemesis Ken's name.'
> 'The CEO foamed at the mouth when he learnt that a former colleague had lured away a client.'
> 'Veer was foaming at the mouth by the time his girlfriend Veena arrived—two hours late—for the date.'

And, finally, here are some lines from a song called 'Mad Dogs and Englishmen' written by playwright, lyricist, actor and singer Noël Coward in 1931:

> In Bangkok at twelve o'clock, they foam at the mouth and run,
> But mad dogs and Englishmen go out in the midday sun.

In the peak summer months in India, I myself would rather stay indoors at midday to avoid sunstroke.

Noël Coward published more than 50 plays and acted in many of them. He wrote and performed many songs, including 'Mad Dogs and Englishmen'. Apart from his talent, Coward was known for what *Time* magazine described as 'a sense of personal style, a combination of cheek and chic, pose and poise'. His comic play *Blithe Spirit* is one of my favourites.

And there you have it, the stories of two phrases introduced by Shakespeare: 'wear your heart on your sleeve' and 'foam at the mouth'.

57

A bird in hand is worth two in the bush / Straight from the horse's mouth

a bird in hand is worth two in the bush

I want to sell my car. I've got a buyer too. He's ready to pay me immediately. But the amount he's willing to give me is less than what I'd hoped for. Should I hold out for a better deal? I could be the richer for it. Or I may lose this buyer and not get a better price later. Perhaps I should tell myself that 'a bird in the hand is worth two in the bush' and snap up the current offer.

The proverb 'a bird in the hand is worth two in the bush' is one of the oldest and best-known in the English language. It tells us to be cautious—to not give up something we already have for something better that we may or may not get. It's advice to curb one's greed and not take risks.

Originally, the proverb may have been a reference to falconry, where the bird in the hand was the falcon. It was certainly more valuable than two birds in the wild that you would perhaps not be able to catch. The phrase is first found in print in English—in an archaic form—in 1450 in *The Life of St Katharine of Alexandria* by John Capgrave:

> 'It is more sekyr a byrd in your fest, Than to haue three
>   secure   bird   fist   have
> in the sky a-boue.'
>   above

A bird in hand is worth two in the bush

Another old-fashioned version of the proverb is found a century later in John Heywood's 1546 glossary *A Dialogue Conteinyng the Nomber in Effect of All the Prouerbes in the Englishe Tongue*:

> 'Better one byrde in hande than ten in the wood.'
> bird hand

The proverb is a calque, meaning a direct translation, of the Latin phrase '*Plus valet in manibus avis unica quam dupla silvis*'.

While the adage came into English from Latin around the fifteenth century, it is likely derived from the seventh century BCE Middle Eastern saying 'Better is a sparrow held tight in the hand than a thousand birds flying about in the air'. This is one of the proverbs of Ahikar. It is from *The Story of Ahikar*, which is considered one of the earliest books of world literature, read all over the Middle and Near East. The protagonist Ahikar was a chancellor to Assyrian kings Sennacherib and Esarhaddon.

And now for some examples of how you and I can use the proverb in our everyday conversations:

> 'Don't leave this club just because you've applied to better ones. They may not grant you membership. A bird in hand is worth two in the bush.'
>
> 'Are you sure you want to break all your fixed deposits and invest the money in a volatile share market? A bird in hand is worth two in the bush, you know.'
>
> 'This candidate is good. I think you should give him the job. After all, a bird in hand is worth two in the bush. If you hold out for an outstanding candidate, you may lose this one and end up with nobody suitable to fill the position.'

straight from the horse's mouth

When you've heard something straight from the horse's mouth, you've got the facts from an authoritative source—from somebody who would know the best or most about the matter.

The phrase likely originated in horse-trading or horse-racing circles. It's possible to gauge a horse's age by looking at its teeth. The expression 'long in the tooth' also comes from this fact. As the horse ages, its gums recede, making its teeth look longer. As age is a determinant of a horse's performance, this is a reliable way to judge the animal's value.

An early use of the phrase in a horse-racing context is from 1861. *Bell's Life in London and Sporting Chronicle* used the term thus: 'CESAREWITCH:—Rank Outsider. A raker to win, straight from the horse's mouth.'

By the early 1900s, the phrase started being used in a figurative way in other contexts. One example is from the 20 July 1900 column 'This Busy World' in *Manchester Weekly Times*:

> "Summer has come at last, and in full force." Thus a sapient contemporary. So nice to be kept well informed, don't you know! If one hadn't the nimble copper to buy one's morning paper, one might have been left in dense ignorance of the fact. I'd a bit of a notion of an idea of a suspicion that the caloric in the atmosphere was constructed so as in many ways not to resemble the depths of winter, but it's nice to be furnished with correct information straight from the horse's mouth, so to speak. [...] Useful things, newspapers.

Here's how you and I can use the phrase in conversation:

> 'The teacher is going on leave. I heard it straight from the horse's mouth.'
> 'Aman and Serena are getting married. I heard it straight from the horse's mouth.'
> 'Read the movie star's autobiography and you'll get the story straight from the horse's mouth.'

58

In stitches (and other related expressions)

Imagine you're laughing hard. Really hard. So hard, you can't control yourself. It could be because of a joke you heard, a funny scene you saw—on screen or in real life—or a comical situation you are a part of. Something that's tickled your funny bone so much you're shaking with laughter; perhaps even aching with paroxysms of laughter.

Another way of saying all this is that you're in stitches.

A stab of pain you feel inside your body—as if you've been pricked by something sharp—is described as a 'stitch'. Sometimes you get a stitch in the side. This is usually the result of heavy physical exertion. But you can also get it from laughing too hard. It's a sharp local pain that can make you double over, much like laughter does at times. Though when we say someone's 'in stitches', the person is usually not feeling a stab of pain from laughing—it's just hyperbole that conveys that he or she is laughing uproariously.

The first recorded use of this phrase is found in Shakespeare's 1602 play *Twelfth Night* (Act 3, Scene 2). The character Maria, who is playing a prank on the lovesick Malvolio, says to her co-conspirators: 'If you desire the spleen, and will laugh yourself into stitches, follow me.' In Shakespeare's time, the spleen was considered the seat of emotions like hilarity. Maria wants her gang to have a good laugh at the priggish Malvolio who is fooled into wearing yellow stockings and cross-garters under the misapprehension that his employer, Lady Olivia, has a fetish for these items. Lady Olivia is, of course, convinced that he is mad.

The phrase has survived to this day without its meaning altered from the way it was used in *Twelfth Night*.

After Shakespeare's use of the idiom, there is a long period when we do not find records of it in print. It resurfaces in the twentieth century though. Here's an example from *The Lowell Sun*, 1914: 'There's a new face among the members in Ben Loring, a natural-born comedian, who seems to have no difficulty whatever in keeping his audience in stitches of laughter and glee.'

And this is how we can use the idiomatic expression 'in stitches':

'Listening to the stand-up comedian, we were in stitches.'
'The students were surprised that their teacher had them in stitches with her jokes.'
'Charlie Chaplin movies always leave me in stitches.'

There are other idiomatic expressions that have similar meanings.

Earlier in the chapter, I referred to something called the 'funny bone'. It refers to a person's sense of humour, as located in an imaginary body part. To 'tickle your funny bone' means to appeal to your sense of humour—to make you laugh. This imaginary funny bone is not to be confused with the real one, which is the part of your elbow over which the ulnar nerve passes. Be careful; being hit in this part of your arm is not funny—it causes numbness and pain in the forearm and hand.

To 'laugh your head off' is to laugh loudly—to LOL, in modern parlance. This idiom is believed to have originated from the execution of Simon Fraser, 11th Lord Lovat (c. 1667–1747). He was a Scotsman, chief of Clan Fraser of Lovat, known for his feuding and changes of allegiance. He was not known to be a nice person. He was imprisoned in the Tower of London in the days leading up to his trial and eventual beheading for high treason—which turned out to be the last beheading that took place in England.

Many people came to witness his beheading at Tower Hill, the place where high-status prisoners were executed in those days. One of the overburdened stands collapsed, killing a number of spectators. This made Simon laugh—even though he was about to lose his own life. This laughter is said to be the origin of the idiom 'laughing one's head off'. The incident also reminds me of the term 'gallows humour' which refers to jokes about unpleasant subjects like death. The gallows is the structure used to execute people by hanging.

Then there's the rolling-on-the-floor-laughing (ROFL) emoji on the internet, usually depicted as a smiling face crying tears of joy while leaning to one side, as if rolling on the floor with laughter. The acronym ROFL was one of the first to find widespread popularity on the worldwide web.

One laughter-related expression that strikes a negative note is 'laughing on the other side of your face'. If you tell someone 'You'll be laughing on the other side of your face if you do that,' what you're saying is that the person will experience a reversal of fortune if they go ahead with a particular action. Their happiness will turn to sadness, hurt or anger. The implication is that this would serve them right. If you tell someone you'll make them laugh on the other side of their face, you're making a threat.

Let's end with a positive expression: 'laughing in the aisles'. This also means 'laughing uncontrollably'. You can tell someone that the speech they have prepared is so witty that they will have the audience laughing in the aisles. Alternatively, you can say that they will have them rolling in the aisles.

The literal meaning is that the audience will find the speech or performance so funny that they will fall off their seats and roll with laughter in the aisles—the space between different sections of seats in an auditorium.

Here's wishing you much laughter in your life. May you often be in stitches. May you laugh your head off. And roll with laughter in the aisles.

59

Cold shoulder

If you look at someone over your shoulder with aloofness or disdain, you are giving that person the cold shoulder. Of course, you don't have to *literally* give that look! If you ignore or snub a person or act unfriendly towards them, then that, too, counts as giving them the cold shoulder.

According to folk etymology, the phrase originated in the practice of giving an unwelcome guest at a medieval castle a cold piece of meat from the shoulder of a sheep or other animal. This was in contrast to guests who were welcomed with hot preparations of prime cuts of meat. This explanation is quite entertaining, isn't it? But, as I mentioned, it is folk etymology—basically, a made-up story to explain the origin of a word or phrase.

The introduction of this idiom is attributed by experts to Sir Walter Scott. Scott used it in *The Antiquary*, a book he wrote in the Scottish dialect and published in 1816: 'The Countess's dislike didna gang farther at first than just showing o' the cauld shouther...'

Scott used the word 'shouther' elsewhere as well. From these multiple references it becomes clear that 'shouther' meant 'shoulder' in the dialect he used. For example, 'They were stout hearts the race of Glenallan, [...] they stood shouther to shouther...'

And 'cauld' is known to be the equivalent of 'cold' in that dialect.

In *St. Ronan's Well*, Scott's novel of 1824, 'cold shoulder' is written the way we write it today: 'I must tip him the cold shoulder, or he will be pestering me eternally'.

An important thing to note is that there is no reference anywhere to the shoulder being eaten. It clearly points to the human shoulder—a cold shoulder that is tipped or shown.

Here are some points that support the theory that Walter Scott's works are the origin of the idiom in English: first of all, of course, his books contain the first recorded use of the phrase. Secondly, he takes the trouble to define its meaning in the glossary of his book. This suggests that it could be an old Scottish proverb that he was introducing to English readers. Finally, within a few years of appearing in his books, the idiom became widespread in its use—finding place in the novels of Charles Dickens, Anthony Trollope and John Galsworthy, among others.

The phrase soon travelled to the US, as evinced by this letter to the editor in the New England newspaper the *Bangor Daily Whig and Courier*, 1939: '[E]minent individuals and his cabinet advisers turned "the cold shoulder" to their ambassador, for his independent act upon this occasion.'

It is important to note here that Scott was a hugely popular writer in his day. So, his inclusion of an idiom in a couple of his books would have been enough to establish it in the language.

In fact, Scott brought many new words and phrases into the English language: 'freelance', 'tongue in cheek' and 'Oh, what a tangled web we weave', to mention a few. He was second only to Shakespeare in this regard.

Here's how we can use the phrase 'cold shoulder':

'Tell me to go and I'll go—but please don't give me the cold shoulder!'

Cold shoulder

'When he bumped into his ex at the restaurant, she gave him the cold shoulder.'

'After her classmates found out that she had complained to the teacher about them, they gave her the cold shoulder.'

60
It's raining cats and dogs

The monsoons have hit the city. It's raining cats and dogs! No, don't worry, there are no animals falling from the sky! Just lots of water. This amusing idiomatic expression implies it's raining heavily.

Frogs and fish swept up by air columns over water bodies are flung into the air and come down with the pull of gravity. There has never been any report, however, of cats and dogs 'raining down' in this manner. Therefore, the idiom does not stem from this phenomenon.

What then is the etymology of this curious phrase?

An email titled 'Life in the 1500s' circulated on the internet in the year 1999. An extract from the email offers a plausible explanation:

> I'll describe their houses a little. You've heard of thatch roofs, well that's all they were. Thick straw, piled high, with no wood underneath. They were the only place for the little animals to get warm. So all the pets; dogs, cats and other small animals, mice, rats, bugs, all lived in the roof. When it rained it became slippery so sometimes the animals would slip and fall off the roof. Thus the saying, "it's raining cats and dogs."

Although it made for an entertaining read, it's an example of folk etymology; it has no truth to it.

So where can the origins of this phrase about feline and

canine precipitation actually be traced to?

The Irish writer Jonathan Swift seems to be the first to use it in print. It's there in his 1738 book titled *A Complete Collection of Genteel and Ingenious Conversation*: 'I know Sir John will go, though he was sure it would rain cats and dogs.'

Most of us are familiar with Johnathan Swift through his book *Gulliver's Travels*. In that book he visits various places inhabited by unusual people and creatures. The most well-known of these adventures takes place on an island called Lilliput, where the people are less than six inches tall. We read this tale as children but it's a satire on human nature, intended for adult readers.

Though Swift's is the first use of the phrase on record, we do not know whether it was he who coined 'raining cats and dogs'. Possibly not.

In 1653, the English dramatist Richard Brome published a comedy called *The City Wit or The Woman Wears the Breeches*. It talks about stormy weather using the line 'It shall raine ... Dogs and Polecats'.

While this writer mentions polecats in place of cats, linguistically the two phrases are similar enough for us to assume that this could have been the precursor to Swift's version.

We may try to come up with logic for why heavy rain is described as a shower of cats and dogs, but maybe it's just a nonsensical idiom people came up with for fun. After all, English people also say 'it's raining pitchforks', 'it's raining hammer handles' and 'it's raining stair-rods' when talking about inclement weather. And if you look at other languages, the expressions for heavy rain become even more interesting.

In French, people sometimes say *il pleut comme vache qui pisse*. That literally means 'it's raining like a peeing cow'. In Bengali, it is *mushaldhare brishti porchhe*. This phrase means 'the rain is coming down like pestles'. One imagines it is inspired by the force with which the pestle strikes the mortar repeatedly when grinding spices. Or maybe the big fat raindrops are the size of pestles! Ouch.

In Spanish, they say *llueven sapos y culebras.* That means 'it's raining toads and snakes'. And in Colombia, they say *están lloviendo maridos*, which means 'it's raining husbands'! Perhaps the song 'It's Raining Men' by The Weather Girls was inspired by this idiom?

And finally, there is this Norwegian expression: *det regner trollkjerringer.* It means 'it's raining she-trolls'.

A she-troll is a female troll. But this is not a reference to the modern-day internet troll—someone who posts offensive comments online to get attention, upset people or cause trouble. The original trolls come from Scandinavian folklore. They were humanoid creatures who were unhelpful, if not dangerous, to humans. A fitting namesake of the internet trolls of today!

Coming back to 'raining cats and dogs'—which might now sound mundane in comparison to some of the more colourful expressions in the other languages—here's how you can use this idiom in sentences:

> 'They've suspended play on the outdoor tennis courts because it's raining cats and dogs.'
> 'It raining cats and dogs out there so I've decided to work from home.'
> 'It rained cats and dogs all night so the roads are bound to be flooded.'
> 'I wear a raincoat *and* carry an umbrella when it rains cats and dogs.'

61

Keeping up with the Joneses

'Keeping up with the Joneses' means buying things in an effort to be seen as being at the same level of wealth or social status as one's neighbours, friends or society in general. Joneses is the plural of Jones, one of the most common surnames in the US.

The phrase originated in a comic strip called 'Keeping Up with the Joneses' which appeared in *The New York Globe* in April 1913. Created by Arthur R. Momand under the pen name Pop, the comic strip parodied the average American's obsession with material goods, solely for the sake of keeping up with the image or status of one's peers.

It featured the McGinises, a family of social climbers who struggled to keep up with their neighbours, the Joneses. The comic strip became so popular that an animated film of the same name was released in 1915. But a bigger testament to its popularity is that its title became an idiomatic expression from the time the comic strip was published.

Marian Mason wrote in a column in the *Akron Beacon Journal* in 1915 titled 'Don't Try to Keep Up with Rich Neighbours': 'There is more tragedy [...] in the common attempts at "keeping up with the Joneses" and the end comes too often in nervous breakdowns, separated families and life under the depressing burden of unpaid bills.' The columnist took a serious look at a topic that Momand dealt with in a light-hearted manner.

The comic strip, which ran in newspapers until 1940,

was inspired by the cartoonist's life in Cedarhurst, New York. Momand and his wife, by their own admission, were newly-weds living beyond their means in one of the wealthiest areas of the US. The characters called the Joneses were based on their own neighbours, with whom they tried hard to keep up!

Momand had originally planned to name the comic strip 'Keeping Up with the Smiths'—Smith being another common American surname. The decision to go with Jones may have been influenced by the fact that the surname Jones and its plural Joneses had been in use since the 1870s to refer to one's neighbours or peer group.

The first example the *Oxford English Dictionary* cites of the usage of Joneses is in *Ernest Struggles*, a memoir of an English station master named Ernest J. Simmons. It was published in 1879. Simmons writes, 'There is a considerable amount of importance attached to this public place of meeting—the railway station. The Jones's [sic] who don't associate with the Robinsons, meet there. Mr. Jones would not like the station master to touch his cap to the Robinsons, and pass him without notice.'

On a lighter note, if the phrase had been coined today, it would probably not be 'keeping up with the Joneses' but *Keeping Up with the Kardashians*! This American reality television series features various members of the Kardashian–Jenner blended family living the high life. Given the success of the show and the number of years it ran, it must have influenced millions of viewers to try to keep up with the family's lavish lifestyle.

There is also an alternate origin theory for the phrase 'keeping up with the Joneses'. Novelist and socialite Edith Wharton was the daughter of American aristocrat George Frederic Jones. Jones, and other members of his wealthy family, owned lavish homes in Manhattan and upstate New York. Novelist Gore Vidal wrote an article in *The Atlantic Monthly* in

1978 in which he mentioned: 'The Joneses were a large, proud New York family (it is said that the expression "keeping up with the Joneses" referred to them).'

However, there is no further evidence to support this theory. During the lifetime of the aforementioned Joneses, there was absolutely no reference to their family being *the* Joneses of the famous phrase. Compare that to the fact that the phrase caught on only after the comic strip was published in 1913.

Here are some examples of the usage of the phrase:

> 'His new car was yet another purchase he made to keep up with the Joneses.'
> 'I've been driving the same car for 15 years because I don't care about keeping up with the Joneses.'
> 'They painted their house to keep up with the Joneses, or rather with the Banerjees.'
> 'It's expensive keeping up with the Joneses, especially when they take frequent vacations abroad.'

62

Beating about the bush / Nineteen to the dozen

beating about the bush

To 'beat around the bush' means to avoid talking about what is important or to avoid getting to the point. It's when you approach a topic indirectly or in a roundabout way. Eventually, one hopes, you get to the issue you really want to discuss and talk about it directly.

The figurative meaning of the phrase is derived from the older, more literal meaning that comes to us from bird hunting. Beaters, the individuals who helped hunters, would beat the area around a bush to unsettle birds so they would be compelled to fly right into the line of vision of waiting hunters, who would either shoot them or capture them with nets.

A version of the phrase first appears in *Generydes, a Romance in Seven-line Stanzas*, written around 1440. It was edited and published by English writer William Aldis Wright in 1878. It goes:

> Butt as it hath be sayde full long agoo,
> Some bete the bussh and some the byrdes take.

The medieval poem mentions directly beating the bush, not about or around it. It seems to say that 'taking the birds' is a superior option to merely 'beating the bush'.

The phrase is mentioned by English grammarian Robert Whittington in his 1520 book *Vulgaria*: 'a longe betynge aboute the busshe and losse of time.'

This is probably the first citation which includes the word 'about'. And here the author is clearly saying that 'beating about the bush' is a waste of time.

The idiom is used again in 1572 by George Gascoigne: 'He bet about the bush, whyles other caught the birds.'

Gascoigne was considered an important poet of the early Elizabethan era. His play *Supposes*, a translation of Italian poet Ludovico Ariosto's *Suppositi*, was performed in 1566. The translation is considered the first comedy written in English prose. And none other than Shakespeare borrowed from it for his play *The Taming of the Shrew*. In Act 5, Scene 2, Bianca has this witty exchange with Petruchio, using a variation on the phrase:

> Am I your bird? I mean to shift my bush,
> And then pursue me as you draw your bow.

Here are some examples of the usage of the phrase:

> 'I know you haven't called me to ask about my health, so please don't beat around the bush.'
> 'Don't beat around the bush—tell me what's really bothering you.'
> 'I know you went through my files. Instead of beating around the bush, tell me what you were looking for.'
> 'If you beat about the bush any longer, your phone battery will die before you get to the point.'

In the last example, I said 'beat *about* the bush'. Using 'about' instead of 'around' is the more British way of saying it. It used to be the more common of the two versions of the phrase but nowadays 'beating *around* the bush' is used more frequently around the world.

nineteen to the dozen

Talking 'nineteen to the dozen' means speaking very rapidly without stopping. It's as if the speaker gets in nineteen words in the time that the average speaker would just be able to speak twelve words. For example, you could say, ' The politician spoke nineteen to the dozen and didn't allow anyone else to get a word in.' Or, 'Get me started on a topic I'm passionate about, like cars, and I'll be talking nineteen to the dozen.'

The phrase is most often, but not always, used in the context of talking. Some other contexts in which it can be used are: 'When I saw the intruder, my heart started beating nineteen to the dozen,' or 'The puppy ran up to the girl, his tail wagging nineteen to the dozen.'

But why the specific number nineteen? Why not twenty to the dozen? That would have been a nice round number!

Well, there's an interesting story behind the origin of this idiom. It is said that the tin and copper mines in Cornwall, in the southwestern tip of England, used to get hit by floods. In the eighteenth century, coal-powered steam engines were installed to pump out the water from these mines in Cornwall. For every twelve bushels of coal, these pumps could clear 19,000 gallons of water. This may be origin of the phrase, though it can't be ascertained due to lack of further evidence.

Another, less common, version of this phrase is 'ten to the dozen'. Though ten is not only fewer than nineteen but also fewer than twelve, it means the same thing, and perhaps puts paid to the Cornish origin theory.

Both phrases, beating about the bush and (talking) nineteen to the dozen, revolve around the art of not getting to the point.

One circles the topic, the other stampedes through it, but in both cases, clarity becomes a casualty. That shared tendency to overwhelm rather than illuminate is what brings them together in this chapter.

63

Steal someone's thunder / Silver lining

steal someone's thunder

To 'steal someone's thunder' is to upstage that person. To pre-empt them in a way that denies them their glory. To do or say beforehand what that person was going to do or say, thereby getting for yourself the attention, praise or success that that person was expecting to get. For example:

> 'Kumar stole Sengupta's thunder by publishing his book first.'
> 'The scientist's assistant stole the scientist's thunder by leaking his boss's breakthrough to the media.'
> 'The airline stole its rival's thunder by launching its international flights three months earlier.'
> 'I did well on my final exams and was about to tell my parents but my brother, who did better than me, stole my thunder.'

Sometimes you can steal a person's thunder without doing exactly what that person was going to do:

> 'Rupak and Mita were going to announce their engagement at the party. But Mita's sister stole their thunder by announcing her pregnancy first.'

This idiom comes from sound effects in theatre. Various methods were used to recreate the sound of thunder in plays. Rolling metal balls down a trough or flapping a tin sheet backstage were two of them. Then in 1704, a drama critic and not-very-successful playwright called John Dennis devised a new, improved method for simulating thunder for his new play *Appius and Virginia*, which opened at the Drury Lane Theatre in London. Dennis's method involved using a large sheet of metal, suspended from a frame, which was shaken or struck to produce a thunderous sound.

Unfortunately for Dennis, his play had a very brief run. Soon after the play shut down, Dennis went to see a production of Shakespeare's *Macbeth*. To add insult to injury, the production had appropriated his invention, the thunder sheet.

'Damn them! They will not let my play run, but they steal my thunder.' According to W.S. Walsh's *Literary Curiosities* (1893), this is what Dennis cried out in the theatre on discovering the theft of his idea.

According to *The Lives of the Poets of Great Britain and Ireland*, published in 1753 by Robert Shiels and Theophilus Cibber, Dennis said it a little differently: 'That is my thunder, by God; the villains will play my thunder, but not my plays.'

In this version, he did not use the word 'steal'. But he was still expressing resentment that his 'thunder' was copied despite his play being shut down.

Dennis's plays may not have gone down in history, but he is remembered for this memorable idiom.

silver lining

Consider these examples:

> 'The silver lining to my flight getting delayed is that I can do more duty-free shopping!'

'He was in hospital for two weeks but he met the love of his life there—the nurse who looked after him. Every cloud has a silver lining.'

'She was incurably optimistic and found a silver lining in the darkest of clouds.'

'The situation was hopeless; it was almost impossible to find a silver lining in it.'

A silver lining is a metaphor for optimism—referring to a positive aspect of a negative situation. It's the bright side of the gloomiest of scenarios. It's a sign of hope in an unfortunate situation. The proverb 'Every cloud has a silver lining' is used to convey that no matter how bad things seem, there is something positive to be found in them. Literally speaking, the silver lining is the shining edge of a cloud backlit by the sun or moon.

'Silver lining' as a phrase was coined by John Milton in 1634 in his masque titled *A Maske Presented at Ludlow Castle*, known popularly as *Comus*. A masque is a form of dramatic entertainment popular among English nobility in the sixteenth and seventeenth centuries. It consisted of masked players acting and dancing. Let me quote from *Comus*:

> Was I deceived, or did a sable cloud
> Turn forth her silver lining on the night?
> I did not err; there does a sable cloud
> Turn forth her silver lining on the night,
> And casts a gleam over this tufted grove.

After Milton coined the phrase, it was often quoted in literature. In fact, such silver-lined clouds were sometimes referred to as Milton's clouds.

The modern-day proverb 'Every cloud has a silver lining' used to have a somewhat different form: 'There's a silver lining to every cloud.' This form first appeared in 1840 in a review of the novel *Marian; or, a Young Maid's Fortunes*, by Mrs S. Hall, in *The Dublin Magazine*, Volume 1: 'As Katty Macane has it, "there's a silver lining to every cloud that sails about the heavens if we could only see it."'

The modern form of the proverb came about thanks to a misprint. In 1849, *The New Monthly Belle Assemblée*, Volume 31, published a review of the same novel, *Marian*. In it, the line was misquoted as 'Every cloud has a silver lining'. This misquote quickly became the accepted version of the proverb. Its popularization was aided by American writer Sara Payson Willis Parton. She wrote a weekly motivational essay for the *Home Journal* under the pen name Fanny Fern. One of her most popular essays, published in 1853, was titled 'Nil desperandum'. It began: 'NO, NEVER! Every cloud has a silver lining; and He who wove it knows when to turn it out. So, after every night, however long or dark, there shall yet come a golden morning.'

May no one ever steal your thunder. And may your every cloud have a silver lining.

64
Can't hold a candle to

This story begins in the days before electricity and lightbulbs. Master craftsmen had to work by candlelight. An apprentice held a candle in a position that threw the maximum amount of light on the object that his master was working on. This apprentice did not yet have the skills or experience necessary to perform anything more than this menial task. Now imagine an assistant even less competent than this one. He could not even be relied upon to hold the candle for the master.

This is the type of scenario that most likely gave rise to the idiom 'can't hold a candle to'. It refers to someone or something being significantly inferior in some way to the person or object with which the comparison is being drawn. Put another way, it means to not be as good as the person or thing mentioned. The following sentences will give you an idea of how the phrase is used:

> 'Pretty as Pallavi is, she can't hold a candle to her sister Ramya.'
> 'Daman can't hold a candle to Goa as a holiday destination.'
> 'Rathore is a good speaker, but he can't hold a candle to Tharoor.'
> 'Alexander McCall Smith's latest book is readable, but it can't hold a candle to his No.1 Ladies' Detective Agency series.'

John Heywood's 1546 collection of proverbs contains a possible early version of the phrase: 'Who that worst maie, shall holde the candell'. Then in 1641, Sir Edward Dering writes in *The foure cardinall-vertues of a Carmelite-fryar*: 'Though I be not worthy to hold the candle to Aristotle.' The wording is slightly different, but close to what we use today. Sir Edward Dering was an English antiquarian and politician. Aristotle, of course, is one of the greatest philosophers of Ancient Greece—few would be able to hold a candle to him.

'Epigram on the Feuds between Handel and Bononcini', written in 1773 by the English poet John Byrom, gives us this rhyme:

> Some say, compar'd to Bononcini,
> That Mynheer Handel's but a ninny;
> Others aver that he to Handel
> Is scarcely fit to hold a candle.
> Strange all this difference should be
> 'Twixt Tweedledum and Tweedledee.

Handel was a German-British composer best known for his musical work *Messiah*. *Mynheer* is a Dutch title of address equivalent to 'Mr' or 'Sir'. Bononcini was an Italian composer whose popularity rivalled Handel's at one point in time. This poem is inspired by the competition between the two.

And finally in 1883 we have the first known use of the phrase in its exact modern-day form: 'Edith is pretty, very pretty; but she can't hold a candle to Nellie,' wrote William Norris in his novel *No New Thing*. Norris was the author of more than sixty novels and many more short stories.

65
Close, but no cigar

Have you been to a fair or carnival where you can win a prize by throwing a ring around a bottle or shooting a balloon? These days the prize is likely to be a stuffed toy. But in the early twentieth century in the US, the prize was often a cigar. If you came close to winning a prize but didn't—possibly because these games were rigged—the person manning the stall would say, 'Close, but no cigar.' While there is no incontrovertible evidence to prove it, this is most probably the origin of the phrase.

A cigar is essentially a rolled bundle of dried, fermented tobacco leaves meant for smoking. The word 'cigar' came into English in the early eighteenth century from the French word *cigare* or the Spanish word *cigarro*—which traces its roots back to the Mayan word *sikar*, which means 'smoking'.

I hasten to point out that in those days it wasn't children who were trying to win the prizes. It was adults trying their luck. And there was little awareness about smoking being harmful to health. In fact, smoking was very much in vogue. And cigars were considered a premium smoke—which they still are among a certain section of smokers.

But our interest is not so much in the actual cigar as in the idiomatic use of the word as a part of a phrase. 'Close, but no cigar' is used to indicate that you came close to achieving success but didn't quite make it, and therefore do not get any reward. A near miss is, after all, still a miss.

It is interesting that long after the tradition of giving cigars as prizes at fairs and carnivals has faded, we continue to use the phrase. Incidentally, cigars also used to be given out by the proud father to relatives and friends to celebrate the birth of a baby. This tradition still exists in the US but is less popular today than in yesteryears.

'Close, but no cigar' possibly came into use as an idiom in the US in the late '20s or early '30s.

In 1929, the phrase appeared as the headline of an article in the *Long Island Daily Press*. 'Close; But No Cigar' was about a man who came second in the presidential race of a community association.

In 1930, the *Cleveland Plain Dealer* described a bowling match thus: 'Peters ... toppled the maples for 120, 100 and 100. Scott was right behind him with 113, 115 and 117. Close—but no cigar.'

And in 1935, in the script for the film version of *Annie Oakley*, we find the line 'Close, Colonel, but no cigar!'

The phrase grew in popularity through the 1930s and '40s and can be found in many newspaper articles from that era.

'Nice try, but no cigar' is a variant of it.

Here are some examples of the usage of the phrase:

> 'It was close, but no cigar for Gaurav as he came second in the annual school exams.'
> 'He caught the ball but it slipped out of his hand—it was close, but no cigar.'
> 'She got the answer to the tie-breaker question at the quiz only partially right. Nice try, but no cigar.'

'Close but No Cigar' is the title of a song by quirky American singer 'Weird Al' Yankovic. Its lyrics include the following lines:

And I told her, I said
Hey! Are we playing horseshoes, honey?
No, I don't think we are!
You're close! (Close!)
But no cigar!

The singer is talking about a girl called Jillian who, the lyrics tell us earlier in the song, uses the word 'infer' when she means 'imply'. And just because of this linguistic misdemeanour, she is almost but not quite the right girl for him—close, but no cigar. Quite a grammar Nazi, this 'Weird Al'!

Horseshoes is a lawn game. Players throw horseshoes at stakes in the ground. Ideally, the horseshoes need to land in such a way that they encircle the stake.

66

In the limelight

A limelight is a type of light that was used to highlight actors on a stage. It served the same purpose as the spotlight of today. The limelight has gone out of use, but the word still survives. When we say someone is 'in the limelight', we mean that the person is in the public eye. In the theatrical sense, it means that an actor is in the spotlight.

The limelight has nothing to do with the sour fruit called lime. It derives its name from the mineral called lime.

Now for a bit of chemistry.

Calcium oxide, also known as quicklime, is produced by heating calcium carbonate, which is the primary component of limestone. When quicklime is heated to a very high temperature, it glows with a white light. This is known as limelight.

A mixture of oxygen and hydrogen are burned through a blowpipe to produce the temperature required to make the quicklime glow. This process can produce extremely high temperatures and care must be taken to keep the temperature below 2,572 degrees Celsius, the melting point of quicklime.

Before the invention of the limelight, gaslight was used to light up the stage and the rest of the theatre, but even when multiple gaslights were used, the illumination was dim; nothing like the incandescence produced by the limelight!

The limelight was first used in the theatre in Covent Garden, London, in 1837. This beautiful bright light was a hit, and its use gradually spread to theatres and music halls all over the world.

While the limelight was an asset for theatre, it was also a potential fire hazard, as it was highly flammable. Many theatres burned down as a result of its use. In 1882, the Prince of Wales nearly died when a wall collapsed because of a fire at the Royal Alhambra Theatre in London.

Not surprisingly, once the far safer electric lights became available in the late nineteenth century, the use of the limelight was gradually discontinued.

The limelight was also known as the calcium light and the Drummond light. The latter name comes from the surname of Thomas Drummond, a Scottish civil engineer who used it in his work as a surveyor. He lit up mountain tops with limelight when the weather was gloomy so he could see them clearly from miles away.

Besides this surveying application, the limelight had a couple of other non-theatrical uses. It was used in lighthouses so that ships could see them from afar. It was also used during the American Civil War to illuminate the enemy.

Let's talk about a luminary who has enjoyed his fair share of the limelight.

Charlie Chaplin spent most of his life in the limelight—in the idiomatic sense. He also acted in a film titled *Limelight* (1952). This movie was based on a novella he had written called *Footlights*. In *Limelight*, Chaplin plays a comedian who's seen better days. The comedian stops a suicidal dancer, played by Claire Bloom, from killing herself. As is evident from the plot, the film is about the dark side of being in the limelight.

When the movie was released in 1952, it was boycotted in the US because of Chaplin's alleged communist sympathies. However, when it was re-released in 1972, it won Chaplin an Oscar! Given that he was born in 1899, Chaplin was basking in the limelight even at the age of 73!

In the limelight

Do you have dreams of being in the limelight? As we have seen, one way of getting there is by becoming an actor. I should mention, though, that not every actor enjoys being in the limelight. French actress Audrey Tautou has said, 'It might seem paradoxical given my profession, but I'm not someone who likes to be in the limelight.'

Here are some examples of how to use the phrase 'in the limelight' figuratively in a sentence:

> 'Renowned Indian actor Amitabh Bachchan shot into the limelight in 1973 after the release of his first hit movie *Zanjeer*.'
> 'Drew Barrymore has been in the limelight ever since her first film as a child actor.'
> 'The award-winning scientist didn't like being in the limelight, so he refused to interact with the press.'
> 'Social media influencers now bask in the limelight that was previously reserved for Bollywood stars.'
> 'Now that the reticent designer is a hit in Milan, he has no choice but to be in the limelight.'

67

Push the envelope / Make the grade

push the envelope

The phrase 'push the envelope' is not about pushing an envelope containing a bribe or a resignation letter across a table. In fact, it has nothing to do with an envelope, the stationery item.

To 'push the envelope' means to go beyond normal or established limits. To be innovative. To do something viewed as risky. To try out new, radical ideas. To be a pioneer.

You could say, 'The clothes Mayur wears push the envelope of fashion.'

While the phrase is used metaphorically today to describe pushing the boundaries, especially in the arts, its original use was in aeronautics, where the word 'envelope' refers to a set of limits such as speed and altitude that it is not safe to go beyond.

The term 'flight envelope' was in use during World War II and its first citation is from a 1944 issue of *The Journal of the Royal Aeronautical Society*. According to the article, 'The "flight envelope" covers all probable conditions of symmetrical manoeuvring flight.' The phrase 'pushing the envelope' is first found much later in a 1978 article in *Aviation Week & Space Technology*: 'The aircraft's altitude envelope must be expanded to permit a ferry flight across the nation. NASA pilots were to push the envelope to 10,000 ft.'

We can credit Tom Wolfe for turning a piece of technical jargon into everyday language. He brought a version of the phrase—'pushing the outside of the envelope'—to the attention of the general public a year later, with his award-winning non-fiction novel *The Right Stuff*: 'In a way they could not have associated with anyone else, at least not easily, because the boys could talk only about one thing: their flying. One of the phrases that kept running through the conversation was "pushing the outside of the envelope."'

The novel was about the Mercury Seven and other test pilots of rocket-propelled aircraft. The Mercury Seven were the seven astronauts chosen to fly spacecraft for Project Mercury, America's first human spaceflight programme, started in 1958. This means that the Mercury Seven were the very first American astronauts. These pioneers truly pushed the envelope.

The phrase is found in the exact form that we use it today in a 1981 *Newsweek* article: 'At 400,000 feet, the shuttle was dropping fast above the Pacific. Since it had no manoeuvring power, the spaceplane had to land right the first time. But even after the shortened flight, Columbia had enough bravado left to "push the envelope" one more time.'

So that's the story behind 'pushing the envelope.'

make the grade

To 'make the grade' means to prove satisfactory, to meet the required standard, to be considered worthy of merit, to succeed. To 'make the cut', 'cut it' or 'pass muster' are other idiomatic ways of saying the same thing.

You might assume that the 'grade' in the idiom means the grade or marks a student gets on a test. But there is a theory that the grade in 'make the grade' means 'gradient' or 'slope'. According to this theory, the phrase originated in the American railways. A train making it up a steep slope was said to make the grade, literally. And this usage led to the later idiomatic use of the phrase.

Here's a citation of the phrase from a 1917 book titled *Making the Grade* by Charles Virgil Mosby. In this excerpt, the phrase is used to describe people who are unfit and, therefore, unable to climb the 'hills' of life:

> A wave of pity sweeps over me every time I see a derelict, human or machine—"could not make the grade" is stamped all over such relics.... Ninety per cent of men and women, normal in mind and healthy in body, can make the grade, can climb the hills if they are properly trained in childhood, and are taught the great laws of life.

Here are some sample sentences containing the phrase:

> 'Sushmita applied for the job but didn't make the grade.'
> 'He wanted to be a dancer in the New York City Ballet but didn't make the grade.'
> 'If you fail to make the grade at this institute, you won't succeed in the corporate world.'
> 'The wedding chef's biryani didn't make the grade and left the bride and groom disappointed.'
> 'Hillary certainly made the grade as a corporate lawyer when she was at the peak of her career.'

68

Have your work cut out / Get the sack

have your work cut out

When you are faced with a task that's difficult or time-consuming, you may say that you 'have your work cut out'. The phrase is often lengthened to say that you 'have your work cut out for you'.

Originally the phrase simply meant that you had a lot of work to do, but later the difficulty of the work became integral to the meaning.

It is believed that the phrase originated in tailoring. The cloth is first cut as per the design of the outfit to be made. Once this is done, the tailor has the task of sewing the 'cut out' pieces of cloth together to complete the job. While this seems like a plausible story about the origin of the phrase, as in several other instances, we don't have verifiable evidence to corroborate it.

It seems counterintuitive that when you have your work cut out, you have a lot to do. If the work is 'cut out', it should be reduced, right? Well, picture the tailor with piles of fabric cut in appropriate shapes for making dresses. Think of the amount of work he must do to sew the pieces together by hand and you will get the sense of the phrase.

The earliest known usage of the phrase dates back to 1591, in a piece printed in London. Here is an extract from the article titled 'A discovery of the great subtiltie and wonderful wisedome of the Italians': '... here is more worke cut out in this one Chapter, then [than] they and their disciples will euer [ever] be able to do ...'

Almost a century later, in 1672, we find the phrase being used in the sense of work being prepared for you *by* someone. This passage is from *Several Sermons Preach'd on the Whole Eighth Chapter of the Epistle to the Romans* by English clergyman Thomas Jacomb: 'I resolv'd to fix upon some continued Discourse in Holy Writ, where I might have my work cut out for me by the Spirit of God from time to time, by which being determined I might be freed from self-perplexing and time-wasting distractions.'

Here the 'person' preparing the work is the 'Spirit of God'. But to understand the meaning we can think of a tailor's assistant cutting cloth as per a given design, making it ready for the tailor to sew.

There is an obsolete French phrase that corresponds to this English phrase. It appears in 1694 in the *Dictionnaire de l'Académie française* or *Dictionary of the French Academy*. The phrase is *tailler de la besogne à quelqu'un* which is French for 'to cut out work for someone'. And it figuratively means to give someone a lot of work. It carries the sense of troubling or inconveniencing someone by giving them a heavy workload.

Do note that the word spelt 's-e-w' is pronounced as 'so' and not 'sue'.

Let's try to use the phrase 'have your work cut out' in sentences:

'The high schooler had her work cut out for her to get admission into college.'
'The Indian cricket team has its work cut out to win the tournament against Pakistan.'

'Given the rising crime rate, the police have their work cut out for them.'

get the sack

To 'get the sack' is a slangy expression that means to be fired or dismissed from one's job.

The phrase is thought to have originated in the practice of workmen carrying their tools in a sack in the olden days. When their services were no longer wanted by an employer, they were handed over their sack of tools and asked to leave. One variation on this phrase is 'get the bag'. Another is 'get the empty'. The latter variation makes one wonder whether the worker even got his tools back when he was dismissed and if he had to leave with an empty sack.

The phrase 'hit the sack' is completely different though. It is of nautical origin and means 'go to bed'.

The phrase 'get the sack' comes to us from the seventeenth century and possibly originated in French. Randle Cotgrave's dictionary of 1611 notes the French phrase as *on luy a donné son sac*, which literally means 'he's been given the sack'. The dictionary explains that it is 'said of a servant whom his master hath put away'. I presume that 'put away' here means 'dismissed' and not 'killed', as it sometimes means in gangster slang. The English version first appears in Charles Westmacott's 1825 book *The English Spy*: 'You munna split on me, or I shall get the zack for telling on ye.'

Here's how you use it in a sentence:

'Sandhya got the sack because she was the most outspoken employee in the organization.'
'Robert got the sack because he made no effort to flatter his egotistical boss.'

'Rupesh decided to pull up his socks and work hard before he got the sack from the new management.'

You could also phrase it as 'so-and-so was sacked': 'The human resources head made a mistake and sacked the wrong person.'

69

Pull out all the stops / Pass the buck

pull out all the stops

To 'pull out all the stops' means to do everything possible to achieve something. To put in maximum effort. To hold nothing back. To employ the best possible resources. To spare no expense. To do whatever it takes to make something happen.

The phrase comes from the playing of pipe organs. These musical instruments have 'stops' (draw knobs) that regulate the air flow. If you pull out a stop, the volume of the music increases. If you pull out *all* the stops, you get the maximum possible musical volume. The result is a full and grand sound. Because of the magnificent sound they can produce, organs have traditionally been used in churches to support choral singing and ceremonial occasions.

The earliest recorded figurative use of the 'pulling out the stops' phrase, in a slightly different form from its current avatar, is by English poet and cultural critic Matthew Arnold. In his *Essays in Criticism*, published in 1865, he writes, '[K]nowing how unpopular a task one is undertaking when one tries to pull out a few more stops in that [...] somewhat narrow-toned organ, the modern Englishman, I have always sought to stand by myself, and to compromise others as little as possible.' Judging from this description, Arnold didn't think too highly of his fellow Englishmen!

Here is an example of the *literal* usage of the phrase from the same year as Arnold's essays. It is from an article published in *The Daily News* of London describing a banquet that took place in the town hall of Birmingham, Warwickshire:

> Such was the clatter of tongues, it was indeed a very Babel. Some idea of the power of the organs of speech (after dinner) may be formed when I say that the enormous organ of the hall was absolutely drowned at times in the storm of chatter that filled the hall. Poor Mr. Stimpson, the organist, had to revenge himself for the loss of all his fine piano passages by pulling out all the stops, and firing a concentrated broadside of all the tiers of his diapason.

Here are some examples of how this phrase can be used:

> 'The police pulled out all the stops to find the missing child.'
> 'Kapil pulled out the stops to make his son's birthday party a memorable one.'
> 'The director said he would pull out all the stops to make the movie a success.'
> 'Louella decided to pull out the stops to do well in her exams.'
> 'The new production of *Macbeth* pulls out all the theatrical stops.'

As you can see from some of the examples, you can drop the word 'all' while using the phrase. You can also use an adjective before 'stops' to make it sound exaggerated and dramatic.

pass the buck

To 'pass the buck' is to shift responsibility or blame from yourself on to someone else. It's to leave a difficult problem for someone else to solve. To put an unpleasant task that you should be doing on someone else's plate. To claim that the unpleasant task does not come under your jurisdiction.

The idiom finds its origins in the card game of poker that became popular in the US in the latter half of the nineteenth century. This was the era of the Wild West and players were often suspicious of each other.

An accusation of dirty dealing could escalate into a shootout, so it was in everyone's interest to keep the game clean. To avoid cheating, the rules dictated that different players deal the cards by turn. A marker was used to indicate whose turn it was to deal. The marker was often a knife with a buckhorn handle, so it came to be known as the buck. Whenever it was time to change the dealer, the buck was passed to the next player in line. And if that player didn't want to deal, he too passed the buck to the next player, and so on.

The idiom made its way into the literary world. Mark Twain used the phrase in his 1872 book *Roughing It*: 'I reckon I can't call that hand. Ante and pass the buck.' This was a literal usage of 'passing the buck' in the context of a game of poker. Incidentally, the expression 'up the ante' comes from poker as well. In this context, it refers to raising the amount of money put up at the start of a game. When used idiomatically, it means to increase the risks taken or demands made in order to get a greater advantage.

The phrase 'pass the buck' became an idiom at the beginning of the twentieth century. An early citation is from a 1902 edition of the California newspaper, *The Oakland Tribune*: 'When the public or the Council "pass the buck" up to me I am going to act.'

US President Harry Truman popularized the counter-phrase 'The buck stops here'. The sign 'The Buck Stops Here' was on his desk, reflecting his belief that *he* was ultimately responsible for every action of his administration. Don't you wish all leaders took responsibility for their actions?

Here are some examples of the usage of pass the buck:

> 'Zeenat took the credit when things went well but passed the buck when things went wrong.'
> 'I'm sick of Arun passing the buck whenever there's a mess to be sorted out.'
> 'During the meeting, the parents passed the buck to the teachers.'
> 'You broke it, you fix it—don't try to pass the buck.'

The two phrases 'pull out all the stops' and 'pass the buck' represent opposite responses to responsibility. Whereas the first phrase is about full commitment and action, the second one is about deflecting responsibility and avoiding effort and accountability. So which one is more you? When the spotlight's on, do you seize the moment or look for the nearest exit?

English, as always, has a phrase for both.

70

Mad as a hatter

In the nineteenth century, hatters—meaning 'hat makers'—used mercury to process the felt for the hats they made. Inhaling mercury fumes affected their central nervous system. The resulting tremors, twitches and other symptoms led to people labelling them as mad. This condition is considered a possible origin for the phrase 'mad as a hatter'.

When you say that someone is as mad as a hatter, you are saying that the person is eccentric or insane. It is often used in a light-hearted manner. For example, you might say, 'If I had to deal with these screaming kids every day, I'd be as mad as a hatter.' Or, 'Some of the outlandish outfits Raveena wears make her look as mad as a hatter.'

And who can forget writer Lewis Carroll's memorable character the Hatter from his 1865 book, *Alice's Adventures in Wonderland*?

In the chapter 'A Mad Tea Party', the protagonist Alice finds the Hatter having tea with the March Hare and the Dormouse. The Hatter keeps changing his place at the table, making personal remarks, reciting poems that make no sense, and asking riddles that cannot be answered. The Hatter's highly eccentric and unpredictable behaviour puts Alice off and she goes away.

Carroll did not come up with the idiomatic phrase 'as mad as a hatter', but he certainly did create this quirky character who was as mad as a hatter! It is believed that his Hatter is based not on a hat maker but an eccentric furniture maker in Oxford named Theophilus Carter, who always wore a top hat.

Perhaps it is no coincidence that the March Hare was a guest at the Hatter's tea party, given that 'mad as a March hare' is another expression with a similar meaning to 'mad as a hatter'. It comes from the way the March Hare leaps about during breeding season. However, the phrase 'mad as a March hare', which dates back to the fourteenth century, is almost obsolete now.

One of the earliest citations of the 'mad as a hatter' phrase is from an 1829 issue of *Blackwood's Edinburgh Magazine*. It appears in a conversation between various fictional characters:

> NORTH: Many years – I was Sultan of Bello for a long period, until dethroned by an act of the grossest injustice; but I intend to expose the traitorous conspirators to the indignation of an outraged world.
>
> TICKLER (aside to SHEPHERD.): He's raving.
>
> SHEPHERD (to TICKLER.): Dementit. [Demented]
>
> ODOHERTY (to both.): Mad as a hatter....

Another early appearance of the phrase is from the 1836 book called *The Clockmaker* by Canadian author Thomas Chandler Haliburton: 'And with that he turned right round, and sat down to his map and never said another word, lookin' as mad as a hatter the whole blessed time.'

71

Once in a blue moon

In the cartoon series featuring the Smurfs—those famous blue characters—the appearance of a blue moon was a sign that a baby Smurf was going to be delivered to the Smurf Village. The phrase 'once in a blue moon' means very rarely, extremely seldom—which would suggest that the deliveries of Smurf babies were few and far between! But is a blue moon only the stuff of comic books or is it a real phenomenon?

The moon usually appears white or off white in the night sky. But there have been rare instances when its colour has looked blue. When the Krakatoa volcano in Indonesia blew its top in 1883, the moon appeared bluish because of the way the ash in the atmosphere refracted the light coming from it. This phenomenon was also witnessed during the eruptions of Mount St Helens in the US, El Chichon in Mexico, and Mount Pinatubo in the Philippines as well as during the Canadian forest fires of the 1950s.

While the appearance of a blue moon is a genuine and rare phenomenon, it is unlikely to be the origin of the phrase 'once in a blue moon'.

A blue moon originally meant something that was impossible rather than rare. Its earliest mention is from an anticlerical pamphlet published by William Roy and Jeremy Barlowe in medieval England in the year 1528:

O churche men are wyly foxes [...]
Yf they say the mone is blewe
We must beleve that it is true
Admittynge their interpretacion.

Here the use of 'blue moon' is sarcastic. It refers to something patently absurd or impossible that church men expect you to believe just because they say so.

From impossible to rare, the change in the meaning of blue moon certainly took its time. Its first documented usage in the sense of a rare event is from 1821. It is found in Pierce Egan's *Real Life in London*: 'Why, Bill, how am you, my hearty? — where have you been trotting your galloper? ... how's Harry and Ben?—haven't seen you this blue moon.' Pierce Egan, the author, was a British journalist and writer on popular culture. This popular work of his was adapted into a stage play.

In the 1823 edition of *Grose's Classical Dictionary of the Vulgar Tongue*, Pierce Egan wrote: 'Blue moon. In allusion to a long time before such a circumstance happens. "O yes, in a blue moon."'

The first citation of the phrase in its current form is found in an 1833 edition of the London-based journal *The Athenæum*. Reviewing an opera for the publication, a critic wrote: 'We are no advocates for the eternal system of producing foreign operas to the exclusion of the works of English composers, but once in a blue moon such a thing may be allowed.'

But we are still no closer to an explanation of how the phrase came to be. To continue our investigations, let's look at a completely different usage of 'blue moon'. The Maine *Farmers' Almanac* has published the dates of upcoming blue moons since 1819. Their definition of a blue moon has nothing to do with a moon that actually appears blue.

Here's the story behind the almanac's blue moon: in a typical calendar year there are twelve full moons. But every few years, there are thirteen full moons in the year. The 'additional' moon is referred to as a blue moon. An American amateur astronomer named James Hugh Pruett misinterpreted the almanac and defined a blue moon as the relatively rare appearance of a second full moon in the same calendar month. His interpretation was printed in a 1946 edition of the *Sky & Telescope* magazine. This erroneous definition of the blue moon became the generally accepted one. But this blue moon is also unlikely to be the origin of the 'blue moon' phrase.

It is possible that 'once in a blue moon' developed from the older expression 'once in a moon'—meaning 'once a month' or 'occasionally'. It was first recorded in 1547 in *The Breviary of Health*, written by Andrew Borde, a physician and writer. In the English of the sixteenth century, he wrote the following: 'Madnesse that doth infest a man ones in a mone the which doth cause one to be geryshe, and wauerynge wytted, nat constant, but fantastical.' Translated into contemporary English by Pascal Tréguer on his blog *Word Histories*, it reads: 'Madness that does infest a man once in a moon, which does cause one to be wayward, and wavering-witted, not constant, but fantastical.'

The word blue may have been added later as an intensifier in the phrase 'once in a moon' to give us the phrase as we know it today. This would be similar to the use of 'blue' in the phrase 'blue blazes'. The 'blazes' in this phrase refers to the flames of hell. And 'blue' is used simply to give 'blazes' a bit more weight. You could say something like 'What the blue blazes are you doing here?' It's a way of expressing surprise or shock. In 1861 Charles Dickens used it in his novel *Great Expectations*. 'What the Blue Blazes is he?' was the line.

Here is how you can use 'once in a blue moon' in a sentence:

'I see her once in a blue moon because she lives far away.'
'Buying the laptop was a waste of money since you use it once in a blue moon.'
'This natural phenomenon takes place once in a blue moon.'
'The neelakurinji flower in the Nilgiri Hills blooms only once in a blue moon.'

72

Don't throw the baby out with the bathwater

'Don't throw the baby out with the bathwater!' You say this to someone when you want to tell them to not get rid of something valuable that's connected to something worth discarding. It's an exhortation to not reject an entire thing just because one part of it is undesirable. Sometimes someone may inadvertently eliminate something worthwhile in the process of removing something unwanted. We use the phrase in that situation to make them aware of the mistake they're making.

Here is how you can use the idiom in everyday conversation:

> 'Why end your friendship with her because of this one disagreement? Don't throw the baby out with the bathwater.'
>
> 'If you withdraw your support for this government because you disagree with just one of their policies, you would be throwing the baby out with the bathwater.'
>
> 'You're getting rid of this car because the air-conditioning is faulty? That's like throwing the baby out with the bathwater!'

A possible origin story of this idiom is found in that notorious email forward titled 'Life in the 1500s'. The story goes that because of the scarcity of water in the medieval era, an entire family had to bathe in one tub of water. The father bathed first, followed by other family members. The baby was bathed last. By this time the water was so filthy you could lose the baby in it and there was a danger of throwing the baby out by mistake when disposing of the dirty water.

This story is fabricated, of course. Nobody in their right mind would bathe a vulnerable baby in such filthy water!

The idiom is most likely a loose translation of a German proverb. The phrase was used by many German writers. Its earliest documented usage is from Thomas Murner's 1512 work *Die Narrenbeschwörung*. The name of the book translated to English is *Appeal to Fools*. In this versified satirical book, the title of the eighty-first short chapter is the German phrase that may be translated as 'To throw the baby out with the bathwater'.

The chapter opens with the following words in German: 'A fool thinks it's not a bad thing to spill the baby with the bathwater; it's as good to leap into hell as to slide into it.' The book is a treatise on fools who, by trying to get rid of the bad, also eliminate whatever good there is. It is accompanied by a woodcut illustration of a lady quite literally pouring out a baby along with the water in a tub!

In 1541, the reformer and theologian Sebastian Franck published *Sprichwörter*, a book of sayings. He explained the 'baby and bath water' proverb with the example of an old horse being sent to the knacker's yard—along with its valuable saddle and bridle.

The first recorded usage of the phrase in English is from 1849 by the Scottish philosopher and German scholar Thomas Carlyle, in his essay about the evils of slavery: 'The Germans say, "you must empty-out the bathing-tub, but not the baby along with it." Fling-out your dirty water with all zeal, and set it careering down the kennels; but try if you can to keep the little child!'

Carlyle was referring to slavery as 'dirty water' and the services provided by the slave as 'the little child'. His point was that slaves should continue to provide the same services but as paid servants. While Carlyle may have been progressive for his time, he would be considered racist today because he believed that black people were born to be servants. I have not mentioned the title of his essay because the word it uses to refer to people of African descent is now considered offensive.

The 'baby and bathwater' phrase was used again in 1860 in an American publication called *The Dial: A Monthly Magazine for Literature, Philosophy and Religion*. It was in an editorial note following an article titled 'On Prayer': 'The defect of the above article seems to us to be that, in the language of a homely German proverb, it throws out the baby with the bath.'

Are you familiar with the cartoon series called *Peanuts*? In a *Peanuts* cartoon published in the *Herald and News* in Klamath Falls, Oregon, USA, in 1959, Linus uses the phrase when talking to Charlie Brown. Little Sally, who hears the conversation, is terrified because she does not understand the figurative use of the phrase. She takes it literally—imagining herself to be the baby being thrown out with the bathwater!

So, if you use the phrase, make sure the people you are talking to know that it's an idiom. Otherwise, they may run away from you—especially if it's a baby!

73

Run amok / Run-of-the-mill

run amok

To 'run amok' is to go crazy, go berserk, go on a rampage. While this phrase has violent origins, it is usually applied to milder situations nowadays—such as children running around and making a mess in the house while playing.

You could say, 'While the teachers were in a meeting, the children ran amok in the school playground.' Or, 'Thanks to the big discounts being offered by the store, the shoppers ran amok.' You could also use the phrase to describe more violent situations: 'The deranged man ran amok shooting at his neighbours.'

But, you might be wondering, what is the meaning of the word 'amok'? And why the unusual spelling?

That's because this word comes to us from Malay. It first reached the English-speaking world via Portuguese. In the latter language, it is spelt *amouco* or *amuco*.

Around 1516, 'amuco' appeared in the English translation of *The Book of Duarte Barbosa: An Account of the Countries Bordering on the Indian Ocean and Their Inhabitants*: 'There are some of them [Javanese] who [...] go out into the streets, and kill as many persons as they meet. [...] These are called Amuco.'

Captain James Cook, the British naval captain and explorer, wrote about his trips around the world in his journals which were later published. He is credited with familiarizing the rest of the world with a version of the old Malay tribal concept of running amok: 'To run amock is to get drunk with opium ... to sally forth from the house, kill the person or persons supposed to have injured the Amock, and any other person that attempts to impede his passage.'

Captain Cook described the amok as a person behaving violently without any apparent cause. The amok would indiscriminately kill or maim people and animals while in a state of frenzy. This would continue till his fellow tribesmen were able to subdue him. At times the amok would end up dying in the process of being subdued.

The Malays did not blame the amok for his actions because they believed that he could not help it. According to their beliefs, he was possessed by the *hantu belian* or evil tiger spirit who made him behave violently without being consciously aware of what he was doing.

As an aside, it has traditionally been taught in schools that Captain Cook 'discovered' Australia. But the Aboriginal Australians were already living there for centuries. So, if anything, *they* discovered it.

While 'running amok' has mostly been described as a culture-specific phenomenon restricted to Java and Malaysia in the eighteenth century and earlier, it is not too different from the violent rampages that people in modern industrial societies go on. You often hear reports of a man killing his entire family before dying at the hands of the police, or someone going on a frenzied killing spree in a school before being apprehended by law enforcement officers. The perpetrators, then and now, are likely to be mentally disturbed individuals.

Amok is also spelt as 'a-m-u-c-k'. And there is a fictitious etymological story of the word involving sailors running a ship aground—that is, quite literally, into muck.

run-of-the-mill

Something that's average or ordinary, not of outstanding quality, or a thing with no special features is described as 'run-of-the-mill'. This is how you would use the idiom in a sentence:

'He was a stylish man and would not settle for a run-of-the-mill ready-made suit.'
'It was a run-of-the-mill movie, but it helped me pass the time.'
'The run-of-the-mill gift he gave her made her feel that he didn't really love her.'
'Your problems are run-of-the-mill compared to his.'

'Run of the mill' was originally a commercial phrase that referred to the output of a mill that had not yet been sorted for quality. The phrase was in use in the US in this sense since the late nineteenth century. For example, an advertisement in *The Lowell Sun* from December 1895 reads: 'Seconds and the run of the mill, but for all wearing purposes just the same as firsts at twice the price.' The products referred to in this ad are clothes from a weaving mill.

The figurative use of the phrase began in the early twentieth century.

Here's a citation from Margaret Mitchell's sweeping historical epic *Gone with the Wind*, published in 1936: '...and I went to work and told them I just knew Jim would rather be buried in my best casket than in some ordinary run of the mill one...'

It is interesting to note that *Gone with the Wind* was the only novel that Mitchell wrote. It won the Pulitzer Prize in 1937 and was made into a movie of the same name in 1939. The Oscar-winning movie starred Vivian Leigh, who was born in Darjeeling of Anglo-Indian ancestry.

Run amok / Run-of-the-mill

Both 'run amok' and 'run-of-the-mill' use the word 'run' in vivid yet wildly different ways—one conjuring chaos, the other ordinariness. Juxtaposing them highlights how a single verb can veer from frenzy to mundanity, based on the company it keeps in a phrase.

74
Rest on your laurels

To 'rest on your laurels' is to be satisfied with past successes and cease to strive for new achievements. It means one has become complacent with what one has already achieved and is disinclined towards making any efforts to achieve more.

In ancient Greece and Rome, people who achieved distinction were honoured with a laurel wreath. This was a wreath made with the leaves of the aromatic *Laurus nobilis* tree, which is also known as Sweet Bay.

The tradition of laurel wreaths can be traced back to the Pythian Games held every four years from 582 BCE to 394 CE in the city of Delphi in ancient Greece. Besides athletic competitions, the event also showcased a range of performing arts. Participants were crowned with a laurel wreath for their outstanding performances in acting, dancing, painting and music.

The Pythian Games were held in honour of the Greek god Apollo, who was associated with the laurel wreath. According to Greek mythology, he was in love with the nymph Daphne. But when he approached her, she turned into a laurel tree. Undeterred, Apollo embraced the tree and wore a wreath of leaves plucked from it.

A coin from as far back as the second century BCE depicts Apollo wearing a laurel wreath. And to this day the laurel wreath continues to appear on medals, badges and other symbols of achievement. That would make it one of the longest-lived emblems in history.

In ancient Rome, the tradition of conferring wreaths was extended to honouring generals who had distinguished themselves in battle. A successful general would parade through the city wearing a laurel wreath. Inspired by this Roman tradition, the nineteenth-century French military commander and political leader Napoleon too was depicted with a laurel wreath in paintings and on coins.

During the Middle Ages and the Renaissance in Europe, great poets such as Dante and Ovid were portrayed with laurel wreaths. The most important poet of a kingdom came to be known as the 'poet laureate'—the poet honoured with the laurel wreath.

Geoffrey Chaucer, who was himself a poet laureate of England in the fourteenth century, refers to a laurel wreath or crown in 'The Knight's Tale' from *The Canterbury Tales*. These are the original lines in the English of his day:

> With laurer corouned as a conquerour
> And there he lyueth in ioye and in honour

In modern English, it would translate to the following:

> With laurel crowned as conqueror
> There he lived in joy and honour

Jumping ahead to the twentieth century, Rabindranath Tagore was considered the poet laureate of India. In another application of the word 'laureate', Nobel Prize winners are called Nobel laureates; Tagore was also the first Indian Nobel laureate. Tagore certainly did not rest on his laurels and continued to be creative in multiple fields right up to his last days.

Here is how you can use the idiom:

'Just because you won a big award last year doesn't mean you can rest on your laurels. If you don't win an award

again this year, you'll get the sack.'
'This brand became the market leader because it never stopped to rest on its laurels.'
'The president was given no time to rest on her laurels.'
'After winning the semi-finals, the captain announced that the team had no intention of resting on its laurels.'

Interestingly, though the idiom 'resting on your laurels' has acquired a negative connotation in modern-day parlance, it was originally used in a positive sense. Here's a citation from *The Gentleman's Magazine*, a London publication, from 1733. It is addressed to a retiring schoolmaster:

> So thou, paternal Sage, may'st now repose.
> Nor seek new Laurels to adorn thy Brows.

Clearly, the schoolmaster is being told that he should enjoy his well-deserved rest and not chase new achievements that may earn him more laurel wreaths. Quite a contrast to the current times that encourage a culture of relentless achievements!

75

A flash in the pan

A 'flash in the pan' is a sudden, fleeting success that is not repeated. It's something that has a showy beginning but ends up being disappointing. In other words, it's something that starts out with promise and then fizzles out.

Here are some examples of the usage of the idiom:

'The '80s pop star's hit single was a flash in the pan; he never released any noteworthy songs after that.'
'The first episode of the show was great. But it was a flash in the pan, as the rest of the season was dull.'
'The athlete showed a lot of promise in the first few games, but, alas, it was a flash in the pan.'
'The huge sales the phone enjoyed when it launched turned out to be a mere flash in the pan.'

One might assume that the 'flash in the pan' phrase originated in gold mining. When panning for gold, a glint in the sediment collected in the pan might have created excitement among miners. But if the glitter had turned out to be something besides gold, it may have led to bitter disappointment.

But, dear readers, it was the pan of the flintlock gun and not gold that gave us this idiom.

'A flash in the pan' originates in the use of the flintlock musket, a type of gun with a long barrel used in the past by infantrymen. This gun was fired by a spark from a flint, a piece of hard grey rock consisting largely of silica.

A New and Enlarged Military Dictionary, Or, Alphabetical Explanation of Technical Terms written by Charles James and published in London in 1802 explains the phenomenon thus: 'Flash in the pan, an explosion of gunpowder without any communication beyond the touch-hole. When a piece is loaded, and upon the trigger being drawn, nothing but the priming takes fire, that piece is said to flash in the pan.'

To explain this further, the bulk of the gunpowder used in the flintlock musket was loaded in the barrel. A small amount of gunpowder, known as the priming, was placed in a little pan outside the barrel. When the trigger was pulled, a spark from the flint kindled the priming in the pan. The resulting bright flame travelled through a hole called the touchhole into the barrel, where it ignited the gunpowder. But at times, the flame from the pan did not go into the barrel, resulting in the gun not getting fired. In colloquial terms, this came to known as a 'flash in the pan' because only the priming ignited and not the main charge of gunpowder inside the barrel. An early documented usage of the phrase is from 1687. English poet and playwright Elkanah Settle wrote in *Reflections on Several of Mr. Dryden's Plays*: 'If Cannons were so well bred in his Metaphor as only to flash in the Pan, I dare lay an even wager that Mr. Dryden durst venture to Sea.'

'Durst' is an archaic form of the past tense of 'dare'. The Dryden referred to here is John Dryden, a famous British poet and playwright.

Another early recorded usage of 'a flash in the pan' is from 'Some Verses Sent by a Friend to One Who Twice Ventur'd His Carcase in Marriage' written in 1703 by the English satirist Thomas Brown:

Then to make up the Breach all your Strength you must rally,
And labour and sweat like a Slave in a Gally;
And still you must charge, O blessed Condition!
Tho you know, to your cost, you've no more Ammunition:
Till at last the poor Tool of a mortified Man
Is unable to make a poor Flash in the Pan.

76
Goody two-shoes

Remember the girl in Class 8 who was teased for being Miss Goody Two-shoes?

A 'goody two-shoes' is a well-behaved person who always does the right thing. There is often a slightly negative connotation to the term though, especially when it's used to describe someone who is self-righteously virtuous. Or a person who's virtuous to the point of being annoying! This person is sometimes also called a goody-goody, and is someone who wants to please people in authority. Someone who wants to let everyone know how good he or she is.

This phrase reminds me of the Mother Goose rhyme 'Little Jack Horner':

> Little Jack Horner
> Sat in the corner,
> Eating a Christmas pie;
> He put in his thumb,
> And pulled out a plum,
> And said, 'What a good boy am I!'

He does seem a bit self-satisfied, doesn't he? But perhaps I'm being a bit harsh towards poor Little Jack Horner!

Let's move on from the nursery rhyme to a song that's slightly more grown-up.

'Goody Two Shoes' is the title of a song by Adam Ant. It was the English singer's debut solo single, released in 1982.

Its lyrics include the lines:

> Goody two, goody two, goody goody two shoes
> [...]
> Don't drink, don't smoke, what do you do?
> [...]
> Subtle innuendos follow
> There must be something inside

It expresses the feeling that people sometimes have about someone who's a goody two-shoes—the fact that they can't really be *that* perfect and there *must* be a hidden negative side to their character.

The earliest documented use of the term goody two-shoes is in English author Charles Cotton's 1670 poem *A Voyage to Ireland in Burlesque*:

> Mistress may'ress complain'd that the pottage was cold;
> 'And all 'long of your fiddle-faddle,' quoth she.
> 'Why, what then, Goody Two-shoes, what if it be?
> Hold you, if you can, your tittle-tattle,' quoth he.

The phrase became popular when the children's story 'The History of Little Goody Two-Shoes' was published in 1765. It's sort of a Cinderella-like story where the protagonist, Margery Meanwell, is an orphan. She is so poor that she only has one shoe. When a rich gentleman gives Margery a pair of shoes, she is so delighted that she goes around telling everyone she has two shoes!

Here's a brief excerpt from the story: 'She ran out to Mrs. Smith as soon as they were put on, and stroking down her ragged Apron thus, cried out, "Two Shoes, Mame, see two Shoes". And so she behaved to all the People she met, and by that Means obtained the Name of "Goody Two-Shoes."'

Later, Margery marries a rich man and ends up wealthy. It was a common theme in children's stories of the eighteenth century that virtue was rewarded with wealth. But of course, Margery was such a goody two-shoes that she believed that wealth should only be used to help others. We daresay a goody two-shoes like Margery is hard to find in today's avaricious world!

'The History of Little Goody Two-Shoes' is quite long, making it a strong contender for the distinction of being the first children's novel.

When this story was written in the eighteenth century, the word 'goody' was short for 'goodwife'—the female head of a household. In the 1870s, the term 'goody-goody' was coined, similar in meaning to goody two-shoes. After that, people started interpreting the 'goody' in goody two-shoes as an abbreviation of goody-goody.

But it was only in the 1930s when people started using 'goody two-shoes' as an idiom rather than to refer to Margery Meanwell, the story's protagonist.

The authorship of 'The History of Little Goody Two-Shoes' is disputed. The story was published without the author's name, but it is believed by many that it was written by the Anglo-Irish writer Oliver Goldsmith—because it was written in Goldsmith's style. Also, importantly, Goldsmith was known to work as a ghostwriter for the publisher of the book, John Newbery. American short story writer Washington Irving also supported this theory. But there are others who believe that the book was written by Newbery himself.

The title page of the book has the following witticism: 'See the Original Manuscript in the Vatican at Rome, and the Cuts by Michael Angelo'. 'Cuts' as used here means 'woodcuts'.

Here's how you can use 'goody two-shoes' in a sentence:

Goody two-shoes

'Amina is such a goody two-shoes; she never joins in with the other kids when they're up to mischief.'
'I'm not a goody two-shoes—I just like to stay out of trouble.'
'You can't be a goody two-shoes in this dog-eat-dog world.'
'Soon after he took over the company, it became apparent that he was no goody two-shoes.'
'You're usually such a goody two-shoes, how could you do a thing like that?'

77
Read the riot act / As pleased as Punch

read the riot act

To 'read the riot act' to someone means to reprimand them sternly; to warn them about unpleasant consequences if they don't stop their unruly behaviour. These days the phrase may be used to describe something as innocuous as a parent scolding their child for misbehaviour. Or, to tell a group of rowdy revellers to not disturb the peace in the neighbourhood.

But it started out with the reading of an actual Riot Act—which originated from a British law—in public, where the punishment for noncompliance was penal servitude, sometimes for life. 'Penal servitude' means 'imprisonment with hard labour'.

The full title of the act was 'An act for preventing tumults and riotous assemblies, and for the more speedy and effectual punishing the rioters'. This act was passed by the British Parliament in 1714 and came into effect in 1715. That was a time of unrest in Britain. The Hanoverian king George I had ascended the throne. And the Jacobites—those who supported the deposed Stuart dynasty—were opposed to King George I. There was a threat of invasion by the supporters of the Stuarts and one actually took place that very year.

The Riot Act was intended to nip any uprisings in the bud. It did so by declaring it a felony if a group of a dozen or more people did not disperse within an hour of an official reading a certain part of the Act aloud to them. The following are the exact words that were read out: 'Our sovereign Lord the King chargeth and commandeth all persons, being assembled, immediately to disperse themselves, and peaceably to depart to their habitations, or to their lawful business, upon the pains contained in the act made in the first year of King George, for preventing tumults and riotous assemblies. God save the King.'

The eighteenth and nineteenth centuries were turbulent times in Britain and public events often turned into scenes of rioting. So violent were the mobs that one imagines it would have taken a magistrate a lot of courage to stand before them and read the Riot Act as this usually resulted in antagonizing the mobs further.

The last time a reading of the Riot Act was attempted was in 1919 at the Battle of George Square in Glasgow, Scotland. Protestors—who were fighting for shorter working hours—snatched from the hands of the official the sheet of paper from which he was reading the Act.

While the Act fell into disuse in the twentieth century, it was in the British statute books until it was repealed and replaced by the Criminal Law Act of 1967.

The earliest record of the figurative use of the phrase is from William Bradford's letters, 1819: '...she has just run out to read the riot act in the Nursery...' It is clearly used here in the sense of a vigorous scolding. Charles Dickens used it in a more literal sense in *Barnaby Rudge*, 1840: 'The Riot Act was read, but not a man stirred.'

Here is how you can use the phrase in a sentence:

'The teacher read the riot act to the unruly students.'
'His father read him the riot act and forbade him from playing computer games.'

'The coach read the riot act to the undisciplined players.'
'An angry Barack Obama read the riot act to the Chinese president, suggesting he needs to be more committed to the protection of human rights.'

as pleased as Punch

'As pleased as Punch' means to be very pleased or delighted. The phrase comes from a traditional, albeit rather disturbing, puppet show called the Punch and Judy show that was popular in England in the seventeenth and eighteenth centuries. Its influence on British culture was far-reaching. Mr Punch was an evil and controversial character who delighted in killing. Each time he killed someone, he would remark with pride and glee, 'That's the way to do it!' The character of Punch was derived from the character called Pulcinella in sixteenth-century Italian commedia dell'arte. A variation of Pulcinella's name is Punchinello, and Punch is a shortened form of the latter.

Another form of the phrase, no longer in use, is 'as proud as Punch'. Charles Dickens used this version in *David Copperfield* (1850): 'I am as proud as Punch to think that I once had the honour of being connected with your family.' Dickens also used the current version of the phrase in *Hard Times* (1854): '"When Sissy got into the school [...] her father was pleased as Punch."'

The earliest recorded usage of the current form of the phrase is from William Gifford's 1797 satires *The Baviad, and Maeviad*: 'Oh! how my fingers itch to pull thy nose! As pleased as Punch, I'd hold it in my gripe.'

Here's how you can use the phrase in a sentence:

'Veena was as pleased as Punch when they told her she was getting the award.'
'The boy's mother was as pleased as Punch when he gave

her a gift on her birthday.'
'I was as pleased as Punch when they served me chocolate ice cream for dessert.'

Punch is capitalized in the phrase because it's a proper noun. However, with the passage of time, it's also become acceptable to use a lowercase 'p' for the word.

Read the riot act. As pleased as punch. One phrase thunders down from the halls of power, the other cackles up from a puppet booth. Whether silencing unruly crowds or celebrating comic chaos, both phrases show how English can be equally at home in law books and laughter.

78

Mind your p's and q's / Fly off the handle

mind your p's and q's

To 'mind your p's and q's' is to mind your manners, be polite and well behaved, or mind your language.

Here's how you can use the phrase in a sentence:

'Her mother told her to mind her p's and q's when they had guests over for dinner.'
'He had to mind his p's and q's in front of his father, who was a strict disciplinarian.'
'Visitors were instructed to mind their p's and q's during an audience with the queen.'
'He minded his p's and q's when he went to meet the parents of his prospective bride.'

The origin of this phrase is not known but one plausible theory is that it comes from teaching children to read and write. The lowercase 'p' and 'q' are mirror images of each other, and young students sometimes mix them up.

The earliest documented usage of the phrase is from the 1756 book *Life and Memoirs of Mr. Ephraim Tristram Bates*: 'Mind your P's and your Q's, and always travel in the Autumn.—Away for Gloucester.—Brother Firelock.—Huzza, I wish I am not robb'd tho'!' As you can see, the phrase is written with a capital 'P' and capital 'Q' in this quote. That's an acceptable way of writing it. It may be written as 'mind your Ps and Qs', without the apostrophes, as well.

Another early example of the usage of the phrase is from a 1763 poem called *The Ghost* by British poet Charles Churchill:

> On all occasions next the Chair
> He stands for service of the MAYOR,
> And to instruct him how to use
> His A's and B's, and P's and Q's.

Another appearance of the phrase is in Thomas Francklin's 1776 play *The Contract*. In a comic scene, one of the characters, Martin, tells his employer Colonel Lovemore, 'Hush—Hush—methinks I hear the rustling of silks, mind your p's and q's, Sir, don't forget your sighs and raptures now for heaven's sake.'

John Williams, under the pseudonym Anthony Pasquin, wrote in *Hamiltoniad* around 1804:

> Would I were metamorphos'd to a Flea,
> I'd hop to Washington, with cruel glee,
> Steal in the galligaskins of our Chief,
> And make his Excellency twist with grief;
> Watch, when he wrote of Diplomatic news;
> And make him careless of his P's and Q's.

The chief referred to here is US President Thomas Jefferson. In case you were wondering, 'galligaskins' means 'breeches' or 'trousers'.

Another origin theory for the phrase comes from the world of printing. In the days of movable type, it was difficult for printers' apprentices to distinguish between the lowercase 'p' and 'q'. This confusion was compounded by the fact that the movable type was mirror-reversed from the final printed result.

One argument that is put forth against both these versions of the theory is that the lowercase 'd' and 'b' are also mirror images of each other and create a similar kind of confusion. Yet nobody ever says 'mind your d's and b's'.

Yet another theory claims that the 'p's and q's' in the phrase is short for 'pleases and thank-yous'. This makes sense as the phrase is about being polite, and saying please and thank you is integral to polite language. However, researchers in the field of etymology have found no sources to back this theory.

Another popular theory is that the phrase is short for 'mind your pints and quarts'. In old English pubs, drinks were served by the pint or quart. The servers would use chalk on a slate board to note how many quarts or pints they had served a customer. So, 'mind your p's and q's' might have been an instruction to them from the manager to keep track of how much a customer had consumed so they could be billed accurately. While this too is an interesting theory, there is, once again, no proof to back it up.

fly off the handle

To 'fly off the handle' means to get very angry over a minor matter or for no good reason, to lose self-control.

This American phrase refers to a loose axe-head literally flying off its handle. The phrase first appeared in print in 1843 in *The Attaché; or, Sam Slick in England* by Thomas C. Haliburton: 'He flies right off the handle for nothing.'

You could say, 'My client flew off the handle when I told him I was slightly delayed by traffic.' Or, 'Vineet was known to fly off the handle and do crazy things.' Or, 'When the boss flew off the handle, it was best not to be anywhere near her.'

Mind your p's and q's. Fly off the handle. One phrase warns

us to mind our manners, the other to mind our tempers. So, whether it's being loose with our language or losing our head like a loose axe-head, both remind us that precision matters—in words and in woodwork.

79
Extend an olive branch

The story of the symbolism of the 'olive branch' takes us to ancient Greece. According to Greek mythology, Poseidon, the god of the sea, storms, earthquakes and horses, and Athena, the goddess of war, wisdom and handicraft, were fighting over whom the first Greek city would be named after. Zeus, the chief deity of the Greek pantheon, decreed that the city would be named after the one who gave it the most precious gift. Poseidon thrust his trident into the Acropolis—a fortified, elevated citadel—and a well of seawater gushed out. Athena struck the arid land next to the well with her spear and an immortal olive tree emerged. She was deemed the winner and the city was named Athens after her.

In Greek culture, the olive branch came to represent peace and victory. The olive branch was used to supplicate or submit to gods or those in power. Also, in the ancient Olympic Games, the victors were crowned with an olive wreath, or *kotinos* in Greek.

This symbolism became a part of Roman culture as well. The goddess Eirene (Irene), the personification of peace, was depicted on Roman imperial coins, holding in her right hand an olive branch or the staff of Hermes.

The Roman poet Virgil used the olive branch as a symbol of peace in his epic poem *Aeneid*. It tells the story of Aeneas who escaped Troy when the city fell and went to Italy, where he ultimately became the forefather of the Romans. Given below are the lines that use the phrase:

> High on the stern Aeneas his stand,
> And held a branch of olive in his hand,
> While thus he spoke: "The Phrygians' arms you see,
> Expelled from Troy, provoked in Italy
> By Latian foes, with war unjustly made;
> At first affianced, and at last betrayed.
> This message bear: The Trojans and their chief
> Bring holy peace, and beg the king's relief."

In the Bible, there is the story of a flood. Because humans have become corrupt, God decides to destroy them with this flood. Noah, the one righteous man, is saved along with his family. He builds an ark and they take refuge in it. At one point, Noah sends out a dove from the ark to find out if the flood is receding. The dove brings back an olive leaf or branch. This meant not only that the flood was subsiding, but also that the divine wrath had been assuaged. And thus, in Christianity, too, the olive branch became a symbol of peace.

'Extending an olive branch' means 'making an offer of peace or reconciliation'. While in Greek and Roman culture people carried a real olive branch to indicate peace or surrender, in the modern era the use of the olive branch is metaphorical. When we say that we are extending or offering an olive branch, we don't actually have an olive branch with us. It would be difficult to get your hands on one in many parts of the world!

Several modern nations feature the olive branch as a symbol of peace on their flags and emblems. For instance, the flag of Cyprus features olive branches both as a symbol of peace and to reflect its ancient Greek heritage. Eritrea also has an olive branch on its flag. The Great Seal of the United States features a bald eagle holding an olive branch in its right talon and a bundle of arrows in its left. These symbols represent that while the US is a peace-loving nation, it is also prepared for war, if the need arises.

The logo of the United Nation features olive branches surrounding a world map.

The olive branch is a symbol of peace in Arab folk traditions too. In 1974, Yasser Arafat, the first president of the Palestinian Authority, brought an olive branch to the UN General Assembly. He famously said, 'Today I have come bearing an olive branch and a freedom-fighter's gun. Do not let the olive branch fall from my hand.'

On the landmark 1969 Apollo 11 mission, astronaut Neil Armstrong left a gold replica of an olive branch on the moon as a symbol of peace.

Here's how you can use the idiom 'extend an olive branch' in a sentence:

> 'After years of hostility, I extended an olive branch to my cousin, but he rejected it.'
> 'The release of the prisoners of war was seen by the enemy country as an act of extending an olive branch.'
> 'As an olive branch to my brother, with whom I was quarrelling, I bought him a ticket to the game.'
> 'The negotiator extended an olive branch to the terrorists, but they did not respond.'

As you can see from these examples, the phrase can be worded in various ways.

I'll end with the haunting words of the singer Leonard Cohen from his song 'Dance Me to the End of Love':

> Dance me to your beauty with a burning violin
> Dance me through the panic till I'm gathered safely in
> Lift me like an olive branch and be my homeward dove
> Dance me to the end of love
> Dance me to the end of love

80
Red tape / It's Greek to me

red tape

'Red tape' refers to excessive and complicated rules, regulations and procedures that hinder the progress of a task. It usually involves huge amounts of unnecessary paperwork. Red tape is often encountered when dealing with governments or large organizations. People also refer to it as 'bureaucracy'.

I recently experienced red tape when I tried to transfer my bank account from one branch to another. It involved visiting both the branches, filling out multiple forms and getting signatures from various people. What a lot of red tape! And such a waste of time, effort, manpower and other resources.

It is believed that (literal) red tape was first used in the sixteenth century by Charles V, king of Spain, who held other titles too, such as the Archduke of Austria and Holy Roman Emperor. He had a vast empire to run. So, in order to speed up the processing of the most important dossiers, he had them tied with red tape—which indicated that they should be discussed immediately by the Council of State. This method was copied by other European rulers to make their administrative processes quicker. It's ironic that the red tape that Charles V introduced to speed up bureaucracy is now the symbol of the opposite—slow, complicated, burdensome bureaucracy.

An alternate theory is that the concept of 'red tape' came

about when Henry VIII sent Pope Clement VII around eighty petitions for the annulment of his marriage to Catherine of Aragon. These petitions were all bound and sealed with red tape.

The earliest mention in print of the literal red tape is from the Maryland Laws (1696–1715): 'The Map upon the Backside thereof sealed with his Excellency's Seal at Arms on a Red Cross with Red Tape.'

The earliest figurative usage of the idiom 'red tape' in print has been found in Edward Bulwer-Lytton's *Alice, or the Mysteries* in 1838: 'The men of more dazzling genius began to sneer at the red-tape minister as a mere official manager of details.'

In *David Copperfield*, published in 1849, Charles Dickens wrote, 'Britannia, that unfortunate female, is always before me, like a trussed fowl: skewered through and through with office-pens, and bound hand and foot with red tape.'

The term was also used by Thomas Carlyle, the Scottish essayist, in his *Latter-Day Pamphlets* (1850). He protested against bureaucracy by describing an official as 'little other than a red tape Talking-machine, and unhappy Bag of Parliamentary Eloquence'.

The tradition of using red tape to bind important files continues in South Asia to this day. You still find documents and paper files bound with a narrow red ribbon in government offices in India, Pakistan and Bangladesh. And, of course, the idiomatic red tape is more prevalent than ever, even in this digitized world.

Here are some examples of situations where the idiom is used:

'There's so much red tape involved in registering a new business, it makes me want to give up.'

'One of the public sector banks has cut red tape by introducing a single multipurpose form that covers many different transactions.'

'They had to contend with a lot of red tape to adopt a child but in the end it was all worth it.'

it's Greek to me

'It's Greek to me' is used when something is impossible for one to understand. Here's how you can use the phrase in a sentence: 'This legal document is written in such complicated language that it's Greek to me.' Or, 'They were having a discussion on coding but it was Greek to me.' A variation of the phrase includes the word 'all': 'Since I'm not familiar with American football, the commentary is all Greek to me.'

Shakespeare used the phrase in 1599 in *Julius Caesar* Act 1, Scene 2: '... but those that understood him smiled at one another and shook their heads; but, for mine own part, it was Greek to me.'

The idiom originates in the Latin phrase *Graecum est; non legitur*, which means 'This is Greek: it can't be read'. The ancient Romans spoke both Greek and Latin. Latin was the everyday language but the educated classes also used Greek. However, by the Middle Ages, the use of Greek declined. At that time, some of the scribes who were engaged in copying precious books were not able to read Greek. When they came across a Greek text, they would write, 'This is Greek: it can't be read'. The text would then be passed on to someone who knew the language.

'Greek' started being applied in Latin to anything that was incomprehensible or unintelligible. And from this sense of the word, we get the English idiom 'it's Greek to me'.

'It's double Dutch' is another expression in British

English with a similar meaning. When you find something incomprehensible, you can say, 'It is all double Dutch to me.' The American meaning of 'double Dutch' is different though. It means jumping over two jump ropes that two people are swinging in circles in opposite directions.

Other languages have expressions with the same meaning as 'it's Greek to me'. Chinese seems to be a language that is considered impossible to understand by various nations. The Greeks themselves have an equivalent expression that translates to 'This strikes me as Chinese'. The Dutch say, 'That is Chinese to me'. The French say, 'It's Chinese', 'It's Hebrew', or 'It's Russian'.

But do you know what the Egyptians say when they don't understand something? They say, 'He's speaking Hindi!'

There you have it: red tape; it's Greek to me. One phrase bemoans baffling bureaucracy, the other, baffling language. Both leave you entangled in confusion. Whether it's forms in triplicate or words that might as well be hieroglyphs, these expressions capture the universal frustration of being muddled and mystified, unable to make any progress.

Acknowledgements

I am grateful to Saswati Bora—formerly at Rupa Publications—who discovered The English Nut and recognized in it the potential for a book.

I am indebted to my friend Sumitra Ray, who helped me in so many ways to put the book together.

And to Gauri Chopra, the assistant copy editor, who went through the manuscript with a fine-tooth comb to ensure that all the facts were in place, I extend my sincere thanks.

Of course, I cannot thank my editor, Kausalya Saptharishi, enough for enabling this book to see the light of day.

References

'A Brief History of Indigo', *The Registry of Sarees*, 7 February 2017, https://tinyurl.com/ffpb4ba9. Accessed on 23 May 2025.

'An Arm and a Leg: Idiom Meaning, Origin, and Examples', *Know Your Phrase*, https://tinyurl.com/j2mchr8y. Accessed on 26 May 2025.

'Apples', *The Youth's Companion*, 10 August 1899, https://tinyurl.com/38khetc2. Accessed on 26 May 2025.

'Assassinate', *Oxford English Dictionary*, https://tinyurl.com/yr6k733e. Accessed on 26 May 2025.

'Audrey Tautou: A Great French Enigma', *Independent*, 8 August 2011, https://tinyurl.com/4pnamhws. Accessed on 27 May 2025.

'Break a Leg', *Wordorigins.org*, 22 February 2023, https://tinyurl.com/58zrdfkz. Accessed on 26 May 2025.

'Celebrate Limerick Day', *Overcup Press*, 1 November 2023, https://tinyurl.com/2p9nkvn4. Accessed on 23 May 2025.

'Drawing the Line in Mississippi', *Library of Congress*, https://tinyurl.com/2zsy35h2. Accessed on 26 May 2025.

'Firsthand Account of Private Prescott Tracy, Civil War POW', *Humanities Texas*, March 2015, https://tinyurl.com/2nmz5msu. Accessed on 18 June 2025.

'Green Color Meaning: Symbolism of the Color Green', *MasterClass*, 4 August 2022, https://tinyurl.com/28h9hekp. Accessed on 26 May 2025.

'Hollywood Goes to Moscow', *Time*, 10 May 1943, https://tinyurl.com/bdh2rnuw. Accessed on 27 May 2025.

'How 1925 Kakori Train Dacoity Led India to a Revolutionary Path for Independence', *The Economic Times*, 14 August 2024, https://tinyurl.com/3hzh6bmd. Accessed on 23 May 2025.

'Is Rh Negative Blood Actually Copper-Based?', *Rhesus Negative*, 26 June 2021, https://tinyurl.com/4tuetekj. Accessed on 26 May 2025.

'Land of the White Elephant', *Siam Rat Blog*, https://tinyurl.com/bmy7ta3n. Accessed on 26 May 2025.

'Loot–Podictionary Word of the Day', *OUP blog*, 28 August 2008, https://tinyurl.com/24rb4wa8. Accessed on 23 May 2025.

'Mind Your Ps and Qs', *Wordorigins.org*, 11 January 2022, https://tinyurl.com/nmjkbstf. Accessed on 27 May 2025.

'More about Break a Leg', *Theatrecrafts.com*, https://tinyurl.com/2b4vna7d. Accessed on 26 May 2025.

'"Oh What a Tangled Web We Weave" Saying Origin & Meaning', *No Sweat Shakespeare*, https://tinyurl.com/53t8w49w. Accessed on 26 May 2025.

'Olympic Basketball's Muddy Beginnings', *Olympics.com*, 28 August 2017, https://tinyurl.com/3nx726nu. Accessed on 18 June 2025.

'Origin and History of *Lemon*', *Etymonline*, https://tinyurl.com/mvcrpvsr. Accessed on 23 May 2025.

'Origin and History of *Sardonic*', *Etymonline*, https://tinyurl.com/2de424h7. Accessed on 23 May 2025.

'Read the Riot Act', *Wordorigins.org*, 17 September 2021, https://tinyurl.com/yyycs28p. Accessed on 27 May 2025.

'Sal Ammoniac', *Oxford English Dictionary*, https://tinyurl.com/59dbaz5j. Accessed on 18 June 2025.

'Sardonic', *Oxford English Dictionary*, https://tinyurl.com/6j84b9tz. Accessed on 11 June 2025.

'Show Business: Noel Coward at 70', *Time*, 26 December 1969, https://tinyurl.com/ywz3y6pd. Accessed on 26 May 2025.

'Silver Lining', *Vocabulary.com*, https://tinyurl.com/3e926z8f. Accessed on 27 May 2025.

'Tamara Ecclestone: Billion Dollar Beauty', *Belfast Telegraph*, 3 January 2012, https://tinyurl.com/yp9zmr33. Accessed on 26 May 2025.

'Tea: A Pagoda Poem', *tsiosophy*, 14 April 2014, https://tinyurl.com/mtaaf7yw. Accessed on 18 June 2025.

'The Hairy History of "Sideburns"', *Merriam-Webster*, https://tinyurl.com/y2zdz429. Accessed on 27 May 2025.

'The Real Teddy Bear Story', *Theodore Roosevelt Association*, https://tinyurl.com/ytmfzsau. Accessed on 26 May 2025.

'The Science & Legend of the "Crocodile Tears Syndrome"', *Madras Courier*, 9 June 2023, https://tinyurl.com/4xtfdp2w. Accessed on 26 May 2025.

'The Teddy Bear', *factoids*, https://tinyurl.com/766b668r. Accessed on 26 May 2025.

'Throw the Baby Out with the Bathwater (Don't)', *Wordorigins.org*, 17 June 2022, https://tinyurl.com/5f3exbyd. Accessed on 27 May 2025.

'Tongue in Cheek', *Literary Devices*, https://tinyurl.com/fu66kttj. Accessed on 26 May 2025.

'What Does It Mean to "Pull Out All the Stops"?', *Merriam-Webster*, https://tinyurl.com/2rfka2nn. Accessed on 27 May 2025.

'What Is the Origin of the Phrase "It's Raining Cats and Dogs?"', *Library of Congress*, 19 November 2019, https://tinyurl.com/3zbdbc6e. Accessed on 26 May 2025.

'Where Does "Run-of-the-Mill" Come From?', *Merriam-Webster*, https://tinyurl.com/4mk57zut. Accessed on 27 May 2025.

'Why Do We Say "Wear Your Heart on Your Sleeve"?', *Merriam-Webster*, https://tinyurl.com/4cy3ps5f. Accessed on 26 May 2025.

'Wolf in Sheep's Clothing: Misadventures in the Land of Fables', *Richard Parkin*, https://tinyurl.com/34cew2cw. Accessed on 26 May 2025.

'Wolf in Sheep's Clothing', *Idiomation*, 15 July 2011, https://tinyurl.com/2p7pbprp. Accessed on 26 May 2025.

'Your "Deadline" Won't Kill You: Or Will It?', *Merrian-Wesbter*, https://tinyurl.com/utckm4rd. Accessed on 23 May 2025.

Al-Khalaf, Nuri, 'Adonis: Selected Poems', *Global Literature in Libraries Initiative*, 21 February 2018, https://tinyurl.com/mvsy7nth. Accessed on 23 May 2025.

Ammer, Christine, 'Beat around/about the Bush, to', *The Facts on File Dictionary of Clichés*, Checkmark Books, New York, 2001.

Arafat, Yasser, 'Yasser Arafat's 1974 UN General Assembly speech', https://tinyurl.com/tfs53u3t. Accessed on 27 May 2025.

Blackstock, Jim, 'The Origin of the Word Freelance and Why It Should Make Us Happy', *Deskmag*, 21 May 2013, https://tinyurl.com/59fyja6n. Accessed on 26 May 2025.

Block, Walter, *Defending the Undefendable*, Ludwig von Mises Institute, Auburn, 2008.

Boström, Mattias, '"Elementary, My Dear Watson"—The Birth of a Quotation', *I Hear of Sherlock Everywhere*, 17 August 2016, https://tinyurl.com/4mufsr4t. Accessed on 26 May 2025.

Brewer, E. Cobham, *Dictionary of Phrase and Fable*, Cassell and Company, 1898.

Brown, Peter Jensen, 'Getting Goats, Losing Goats, Stable Goats and Navy Goats—a History and Etymology of "Get My Goat"', *Early Sports and Pop Culture History Blog*, 9 October 2014, https://tinyurl.com/ycct9t27. Accessed on 26 May 2025.

Bullen, Ross, 'Race and the White Elephant War of 1884', *Bunk History*, 11 October 2017, https://tinyurl.com/3ty3239x. Accessed on 26 May 2025.

Burch, Michael R., 'The Best Doggerel of All Time', *The HyperTexts*, https://tinyurl.com/7ayfdkxc. Accessed on 23 May 2025.

Carey, Stan, 'Explaining "Fell" in "One Fell Swoop"', *Vocabulary.com*, https://tinyurl.com/mr3ar8ee. Accessed on 26 May 2025.

Carlyle, Thomas, *Latter-Day Pamphlets*, Chapman and Hall, London, 1850.

Cotgrave, Randle, *A Dictionarie of the French and English Tongues*, Adam Islip, London, 1611.

Cunningham, John M., 'Did Marie-Antoinette Really Say "Let Them Eat Cake"?', *Britannica*, https://tinyurl.com/bdfsxww5. Accessed on 26 May 2025.

Cutolo, Morgan, 'What Does the Saying "Close, but No Cigar" Really Mean?', *Reader's Digest*, 26 June 2024, https://tinyurl.com/r4x3csa5. Accessed on 27 May 2025.

De Graaf, Jack, 'The Fascinating Origins of the Word "Boycott"', *The Fact Site*, 24 May 2019, https://tinyurl.com/vfx8kurv. Accessed on 23 May 2025.

Dhillon, Amrit, 'The Funny Thing about India Is That So Many Don't See the Funny Side', *The National*, 7 February 2015, https://tinyurl.com/yazxrh8k. Accessed on 26 May 2025.

Dickens, Charles, *David Copperfield*, Bradbury & Evans, London, 1850.

Dickens, Charles, *Great Expectations*, Estes and Lauriat, Boston, 1881.

Dickens, Charles, *Hard Times and Reprinted Pieces*, Chapman and Hall, London, 1905.

Doctor, Vikram, 'Khaki: Celebrating the Unexpected Success of an Indian Colour', *The Economic Times*, 7 July 2018, https://tinyurl.com/2bduefms. Accessed on 23 May 2025.

Egan, Pierce, *Real Life in London*, Methuen & Co., London, 1905.

Engle, Paul, 'Sal Ammoniac', *Conciatore*, 14 August 2015, https://tinyurl.com/2hfkfbu3. Accessed on 18 June 2025.

Farmer, John S., *Americanisms—Old & New: A Dictionary of Words, Phrases and Colloquialisms*, Thomas Poulter & Sons, London, 1889.

Graziosi, Marco, 'The Limerick', *Edward Lear's Nonsense Poetry and Art*, 19 October 2022, https://tinyurl.com/mw4ukcj5. Accessed on 23 May 2025.

Hall, Sheldon, 'Pass the Ammunition: A Short Etymology of "Blockbuster"', *The Return of the Epic Film: Genre, Aesthetics and History in the 21st Century*, Andrew Elliot (ed.), Edinburgh University Press, 2014, pp. 147–166.

Hannikainen, Diana, 'The Moon Is "Blue" This Wednesday...or Is It?', *Sky & Telescope*, 29 August 2023, https://tinyurl.com/49292wky. Accessed on 27 May 2025.

Harness, Jill, 'Where Did the Graveyard Shift Come From', *Chron*, https://tinyurl.com/2vk6sumh. Accessed on 26 May 2025.

Hiskey, Daven, 'What's the Origin of the Phrase "Run Amok"?', *Mental Floss*, 29 August 2013, https://tinyurl.com/yt867zzz. Accessed on 27 May 2025.

Hiskey, Daven, 'Where Did the Phrase "Caught Red Handed" Come From?', *Mental Floss*, 16 January 2013, https://tinyurl.com/3ue49dfn. Accessed on 26 May 2025.

Hussain, Mehwash, 'The Story behind the Term "Blockbuster"', *The Hindu*, 5 December 2024, https://tinyurl.com/539sb3y8. Accessed on 27 May 2025.

Johnson, Vanessa, 'Cat or Hare', *don Quijote blog*, 29 April 2019, https://tinyurl.com/29yrrs3e. Accessed on 16 June 2025.

Kale, Sharwari, 'From Chaturanga to Chess—The History of the Origin of Chess', *Homegrown*, 8 June 2021, https://tinyurl.com/yjxrwk5w. Accessed on 23 May 2025.

Karpinski, Anna, '14 Common English Idioms: Meanings, Fun Facts & Examples', *Owlcation*, 12 November 2023, https://tinyurl.com/37xcwtrz. Accessed on 26 May 2025.

Kelly, John, 'The Etymological Underworld of "Phony"', *Mashed*

Radish, 8 March 2016, https://tinyurl.com/5n9y5zay. Accessed on 27 May 2025.

Klein, Christopher, '10 Ways Shakespeare Changed the Way You Talk', *History*, 22 April 2024, https://tinyurl.com/b27jfk3c. Accessed on 26 May 2025.

Lawrence, George Alfred, *Guy Livingstone; or, "Thorough."*, Harper & Brothers, New York, 1868.

Liberman, Anatoly, 'Bare or Bear, or, the Story of Berserk', *OUP blog*, 20 August 2008, https://tinyurl.com/yh7vvevw. Accessed on 23 May 2025.

Livingston, Stephenie, 'History Re-written: Christopher Columbus and the Cannibals', *Florida Museum*, 9 March 2015, https://tinyurl.com/5n6ru6ca. Accessed on 23 May 2025.

Mair, George, and Carla Jenkins, 'Why Last Man Beheaded in Britain Was Not a "Terrible Auld Monster"', *The Times*, 10 April 2025, https://tinyurl.com/yy4cwpna. Accessed on 26 May 2025.

Manges, Zach, 'Writing Limericks: A How-To and a History', *The Saturday Evening Post*, 24 April 2017, https://tinyurl.com/yc2ah7px. Accessed on 23 May 2025.

Martin, Gary, 'A Bird in the Hand Is Worth Two in the Bush', *Phrase Finder*, https://tinyurl.com/5xs25pxv. Accessed on 26 May 2025.

Martin, Gary, 'A Dead Ringer', *Phrase Finder*, https://tinyurl.com/bdf9d8f5. Accessed on 26 May 2025.

Martin, Gary, 'An Arm and a Leg', *Phrase Finder*, https://tinyurl.com/4msxv77c. Accessed on 26 May 2025.

Martin, Gary, 'As Mad as a Hatter', *Phrase Finder*, https://tinyurl.com/mwj6a9vs. Accessed on 27 May 2025.

Martin, Gary, 'Barking Up the Wrong Tree', *Phrase Finder*, https://tinyurl.com/2hamjuf7. Accessed on 26 May 2025.

Martin, Gary, 'Beat around the Bush', *Phrase Finder*, https://tinyurl.com/3nm76b7v. Accessed on 26 May 2025.

Martin, Gary, 'Blue Blood', *Phrase Finder*, https://tinyurl.com/4rwxfmjy. Accessed on 26 May 2025.

Martin, Gary, 'Break a Leg', *Phrase Finder*, https://tinyurl.com/bdhwr74j. Accessed on 26 May 2025.

Martin, Gary, 'Cat Got Your Tongue?', *Phrase Finder*, https://tinyurl.com/4tets5hf. Accessed on 26 May 2025.

Martin, Gary, 'Cold Shoulder', *Phrase Finder*, https://tinyurl.com/4btb5a36. Accessed on 26 May 2025.

Martin, Gary, 'Crocodile Tears', *Phrase Finder*, https://tinyurl.com/mry3c5r4. Accessed on 26 May 2025.

Martin, Gary, 'Every Cloud Has a Silver Lining', *Phrase Finder*, https://tinyurl.com/yc4ven8h. Accessed on 27 May 2025.

Martin, Gary, 'Flash in the Pan', *Phrase Finder*, https://tinyurl.com/3ftmah25. Accessed on 27 May 2025.

Martin, Gary, 'Fly Off the Handle', *Phrase Finder*, https://tinyurl.com/59ubvb49. Accessed on 27 May 2025.

Martin, Gary, 'Foam at the Mouth', *Phrase Finder*, https://tinyurl.com/y4xcejhp. Accessed on 26 May 2025.

Martin, Gary, 'Get the Sack', *Phrase Finder*, https://tinyurl.com/yey9jz25. Accessed on 27 May 2025.

Martin, Gary, 'Graveyard Shift', *Phrase Finder*, https://tinyurl.com/4yshv894. Accessed on 26 May 2025.

Martin, Gary, 'Hold a Candle', *Phrase Finder*, https://tinyurl.com/33w8n276. Accessed on 27 May 2025.

Martin, Gary, 'In Stitches', *Phrase Finder*, https://tinyurl.com/bdfebsvd. Accessed on 26 May 2025.

Martin, Gary, 'Pass the Buck', *Phrase Finder*, https://tinyurl.com/2ev855nk. Accessed on 27 May 2025.

Martin, Gary, 'Push the Envelope', *Phrase Finder*, https://tinyurl.com/3c3bknk4. Accessed on 27 May 2025.

Martin, Gary, 'Red Tape', *Phrase Finder*, https://tinyurl.com/56fca6xn. Accessed on 27 May 2025.

Martin, Gary, 'Rest on Your Laurels', *Phrase Finder*, https://tinyurl.com/3hm5un2z. Accessed on 27 May 2025.

Mayer, Johanna, 'The Origin of the Word "Quarantine"', *Science Friday*, 4 September 2018, https://tinyurl.com/4nuk9ejc. Accessed on 23 May 2025.

Meyer, Edward, *Machiavelli and the Elizabethan Drama*, Verlag von Emil Felber, Weimar, 1897.

McCorquodale, Amanda, 'Where Does the Expression "Crocodile Tears" Come From?', *Mental Floss*, 14 June 2016, https://tinyurl.com/37b9x3x9. Accessed on 26 May 2025.

Mikkelson, Barbara, 'Life in the 1500s', *Snopes*, 16 December 2000, https://tinyurl.com/3j64hmxy. Accessed on 26 May 2025.

Miss Celania, 'Khakis: A Heat Stroke of Genius', *Neatorama*, 27 August 2012, https://tinyurl.com/ynazv4pf. Accessed on 23 May 2025.

Morton, Ella, 'What It Actually Means to "Read the Riot Act" to Someone', *Atlas Obscura*, 28 July 2022, https://tinyurl.com/2c5fcyk8. Accessed on 27 May 2025.

Mosby, Charles Virgil, *Making the Grade*, Highland Press, 1917.

Naismith, James, *Basketball: Its Origin and Development*, Association Press, New York, 1941.

Newton, Isaac, 'A letter of Mr. Isaac Newton, Professor of the Mathematicks in the University of Cambridge; containing his new theory about light and colors: sent by the author to the publisher from Cambridge, Febr. 6. 1671/72; in order to be communicated to the R. Society', *Philosophical Transactions of the Royal Society*, No. 80, 19 February 1672, pp. 3075–3087, https://tinyurl.com/5eke2j32. Accessed on 11 June 2025.

Nix, Elizabeth, 'Where Did the Phrase "Mad as a Hatter" Come From?', *History*, 24 January 2025, https://tinyurl.com/3svhc67s. Accessed on 27 May 2025.

Nosowitz, Dan, 'It's All Greek to You and Me, so What Is It to the Greeks?', *Atlas Obscura*, 8 August 2019, https://tinyurl.com/y97b8mdm. Accessed on 27 May 2025.

O'Conner, Patricia T., and Stewart Kellerman, 'A Phony Etymology', *Grammarphobia*, 25 March 2019, https://tinyurl.com/5n9axzt4. Accessed on 17 June 2025.

O'Conner, Patricia T., and Stewart Kellerman, 'Are Your Ears Burning?', *Grammarphobia*, 1 June 2018, https://tinyurl.com/36uyxwz7. Accessed on 26 May 2025.

O'Conner, Patricia T., and Stewart Kellerman, 'Hair of the Dog', *Grammarphobia*, 31 December 2018, https://tinyurl.com/yz6scmr4. Accessed on 26 May 2025.

O'Conner, Patricia T., and Stewart Kellerman, 'Keeping Up with the Joneses', *Grammarphobia*, 18 January 2017, https://tinyurl.com/nwf24c6k. Accessed on 26 May 2025.

O'Conner, Patricia T., and Stewart Kellerman, 'Let's Play It by Ear', *Grammarphobia*, 29 August 2013, https://tinyurl.com/5ar2zawy. Accessed on 26 May 2025.

O'Conner, Patricia T., and Stewart Kellerman, 'Pleased as Punch', *Grammarphobia*, 21 February 2008, https://tinyurl.com/32c8ajze. Accessed on 27 May 2025.

Otis, Daniel, 'In the Abode of Kings', *Southeast Asia Globe*, 15 July 2013, https://tinyurl.com/4m6uwtd9. Accessed on 26 May 2025.

Quinion, Michael, 'Blue Blood', *World Wide Words*, 20 November 1999, https://tinyurl.com/ppw5e8ru. Accessed on 26 May 2025.

Quinion, Michael, 'Don't Throw the Baby Out with the Bathwater', *World Wide Words*, 13 April 2013, https://tinyurl.com/mukacvk4. Accessed on 27 May 2025.

Quinion, Michael, 'Goody Two Shoes', *World Wide Words*, 13 December 2008, https://tinyurl.com/543vta4t. Accessed on 27 May 2025.

Quinion, Michael, 'The Lure of the Red Herring', *World Wide Words*, 25 October 2008, https://tinyurl.com/yztknswp. Accessed on 26 May 2025.

Quinion, Michael, 'Work Cut Out', *World Wide Words*, 25 March 2006, https://tinyurl.com/yemmenaw. Accessed on 27 May 2025.

Roy, Parama, 'Discovering India, Imagining *Thuggee*', *Indian Traffic: Identities in Question in Colonial and Postcolonial India*, University of California Press, California, 1998.

Saddan, Nitsan, 'Rockets, Pilots and Mishaps: The Story behind Murphy's Law', *CTech by Calcalist*, 28 June 2020, https://tinyurl.com/333vu6v6. Accessed on 26 May 2025.

Saint Martin, Manuel L., 'Running Amok: A Modern Perspective on a Culture-Bound Syndrome', *Primary Care Companion to the Journal of Clinical Psychiatry*, Vol. 1, No. 3, 1999, pp. 66–70, https://tinyurl.com/48jvuwsn. Accessed on 27 May 2025.

Smith, Kate, 'The Colorful Connection between Blue Blood & Silver Spoon', *Sensational Color*, https://tinyurl.com/yv3zddzj. Accessed on 26 May 2025.

Sobel, Bernard (ed.), *The Theatre Handbook and Digest of Plays*, Crown Publishers, 1940.

Soniak, Matt, 'What's the Origin of "Let the Cat Out of the Bag"?', *Mental Floss*, 29 December 2020, https://tinyurl.com/45a9nupd. Accessed on 26 May 2025.

Tearle, Dr Oliver, 'A Summary and Analysis of the Fable of "The Wolf in Sheep's Clothing"', *Interesting Literature*, https://tinyurl.com/2k9f33ym. Accessed on 16 June 2025.

Tien, David Robbins, 'Chinese Origin of the Term Pagoda: Liang Sicheng's Proposed Etymology', *Acta Orientalia*, Vol. 77, 2016, https://tinyurl.com/mkx2ms7h. Accessed on 23 May 2025.

Tréguer, Pascal, '"To Pull Out All the Stops": Meaning and Origin', *word histories*, https://tinyurl.com/4j79scee. Accessed on 27 May 2025.

Tréguer, Pascal, 'Meaning and Origin of "To Be Barking Up the Wrong Tree"', *word histories*, https://tinyurl.com/3awmdcdh. Accessed on 26 May 2025.

Tréguer, Pascal, 'Meaning and Origin of "To Keep Up with the Joneses"', *word histories*, https://tinyurl.com/j54485d6. Accessed on 26 May 2025.

Tréguer, Pascal, 'Meaning and Origin of "To Steal Someone's Thunder"', *word histories*, https://tinyurl.com/4xtrwxdv. Accessed on 27 May 2025.

Tréguer, Pascal, 'Origin of "An Apple a Day Keeps the Doctor Away"', *word histories*, https://tinyurl.com/mrnxv5rr. Accessed on 26 May 2025.

Tréguer, Pascal, 'Origin of "Flash in the Pan" and of the French Verb "Rater"', *word histories*, https://tinyurl.com/ymmxw6wp. Accessed on 27 May 2025.

Tréguer, Pascal, 'Origin of the Phrase "Straight from the Horse's Mouth"', *word histories*, https://tinyurl.com/5ycmjny2. Accessed on 26 May 2025.

Tréguer, Pascal, 'The Authentic Origin of "Once in a Blue Moon"', *word histories*, https://tinyurl.com/4pv45r43. Accessed on 27 May 2025.

Tréguer, Pascal, 'The Authentic Origin of "to Bite the Bullet"', *word histories*, https://tinyurl.com/v79yyt7m. Accessed on 26 May 2025.

Tréguer, Pascal, 'The Curious History of the Word "Gossip"', *word histories*, https://tinyurl.com/barfkfe3. Accessed on 23 May 2025.

Tréguer, Pascal, 'The German Origin of the Phrase "To Throw the Baby Out with the Bathwater"', *word histories*, https://tinyurl.com/2saffccs. Accessed on 27 May 2025.

Tréguer, Pascal, 'The Mistaken Origin of "White Elephant" in the Oxford English Dictionary', *word histories*, https://tinyurl.com/zsca4k6a. Accessed on 26 May 2025.

Tréguer, Pascal, 'The Supposed Origin of "To Have One's Work Cut Out"', *word histories*, https://tinyurl.com/bdfedhm3. Accessed on 27 May 2025.

Twain, Mark, *Roughing It*, American Publishing Company, 1872.

Upton, Emily, 'The Origin of the Phrase "Close, but No Cigar"', *Today I Found Out*, 16 September 2013, https://tinyurl.com/2kth3mds. Accessed on 27 May 2025.

Upton, Emily, 'The Origin of the Phrase "Once in a Blue Moon"', *Today I Found Out*, 10 June 2013, https://tinyurl.com/54w3tk7h. Accessed on 27 May 2025.

Upton, George, 'Make Lemonade: A Motto and a Method', *Kinfolk*, Issue 44, 2022, https://tinyurl.com/4f2auwzj. Accessed on 11 June 2025.

Waldron, H.A., 'Did the Mad Hatter Have Mercury Poisoning', *British Medical Journal (Clinical Research Ed.)*, Vol. 287, 1983, p. 1961, https://tinyurl.com/4zze79ab. Accessed on 27 May 2025.

Wilkes, Jonny, 'Why Do We Say "Raining Cats and Dogs"?', *History Extra*, 13 January 2022, https://tinyurl.com/kpvb7ax6. Accessed on 26 May 2025.

Willard, Jim, 'John Dennis Was First to Have His Thunder Stolen', *Loveland Reporter-Herald*, 27 March 2018, https://tinyurl.com/yymzuzhy. Accessed on 27 May 2025.

Withington, John, *Assassins' Deeds: A History of Assassination from Ancient Egypt to the Present Day*, Reaktion Books, London, 2020.

Young, Sam, 'An Arm and a Leg', *Sam Young*, 23 May 2012, https://tinyurl.com/mrypfp3y. Accessed on 26 May 2025.

Zimmer, Ben, '"Getting One's Goat": Can You Help Solve the Mystery?', *Visual Thesaurus*, 17 November 2014, https://tinyurl.com/yeys36td. Accessed on 18 June 2025.

www.ingramcontent.com/pod-product-compliance
Lightning Source LLC
Chambersburg PA
CBHW020832160426
43192CB00007B/618